THE
FAMILY
CHRISTMAS
BOOK

# THE
# FAMILY
# CHRISTMAS
# BOOK

## Barbara Rinkoff

Doubleday & Company, Inc., Garden City, New York

To my son Bob

# CONTENTS

# INTRODUCTION

Christmas is a family time. Not only a time to share in the celebration, but a time to share the fun and anticipation of getting ready for Christmas.

Having three children of my own, and all of us being of an arts and craftsy nature, I am always on the lookout for new ideas, especially at holiday times. And so this book really began when I tried to locate information on Christmas customs around the world, decorations and gifts that my children and I could make, and recipes for some new tantalizing Christmas foods to make our holiday more enjoyable.

First, let me say that I like reading and "thumbing" on the chaise longue in my bedroom. As I started collecting Christmas material, the pile of books and magazines began to take on gigantic proportions. Soon the stacks began to teeter precariously. Before long, getting past the chaise was like running an obstacle course. The family dubbed the stacks "Mother's Christmas Mountains," and they were! If you have ever tried to locate this material, I am sure that you know what I mean.

The more I read, the more my notes grew. And then one day my daughter said, "It must be a pain having to wade through all that just to get the information you want." I had to agree.

My feeling was that, if I had so much trouble going through material to find what I was looking for, others must be sharing my dilemma. I began to think how much easier it would be if the information could be under one cover. Right then and there *The Family Christmas Book* was born.

In this book you will find Christmas lore; the origin of symbols; celebrations and traditions in other countries, some of which you might enjoy incorporating into your own celebration; ideas and simple instructions for young and old in making decorations and gifts; recipes for cooking and baking tempting dishes for your own table and for gift giving; international games for Christmas; and an around-the-world, mail order shopping guide for those of us who haven't the time to fuss or shop.

Let the children help. My own were more delighted with the tiny plastic table-top trees from the five-and-dime, which they adorned with their own creations, than they were with the family tree with store-bought decorations. And though purchased gifts are lovely, what parent or grandparent isn't more touched by something made especially for him by a child? Here is a time to do things with your children. My own experience has been that letting them help in planning, decorating, making things, and acting as host makes Christmas a memorable and exciting family experience.

Friends, too, are delighted with a box of gaily Christmas-wrapped homemade cookies, candy, or jams. "To think that you took the time!" as a friend of mine said recently. In these days of rush and commercialism, a special thought and a personal effort mean a lot.

So preparing for Christmas can be fun for the whole family. The special magic of doing things together will make the occasion something to remember for years to come.

# INTERNATIONAL CHRISTMAS
# SHOPPING BY MAIL ORDER

As you read through this book, certain questions will probably occur to you. For instance, where do you get beeswax for making candles? Can you buy foreign candies somewhere, since you haven't time to prepare them? How can you make some of those foreign cookies without proper utensils? Forget your worries; you will find the answer if you browse through my mail order shopping guide. No longer is there a need to give up the attempt at a Christmas with a foreign flavor because of lack of time or ability to make or create foreign dishes, decorations, or gifts.

These fascinating pages will tell you where to get everything from foreign utensils to delicious taste treats from other lands. Also, there are exotic and unusual gifts from all over the world for your family, friends, and household. In fact, once you start sending for catalogues and thumbing through them you will wonder how you ever managed to shop without them.

I have included catalogues from the United States and abroad. You will find many foreign items are available through shops in the United States, which makes arranging for their receipt a great deal easier and faster. If you find items listed in this book that you cannot readily locate in your local stores, refer to the guide. Check where to purchase English fruitcakes, Italian candy, Christmas cards designed by artists in other countries, gift wrap supplies, foreign toys, a Santa Piñata, a gingerbread house, German tree ornaments, wood carvings, Christmas charms, arts and crafts supplies, and many other foods, utensils, decorations, favors, games, and gifts.

Just reading through the guide will spark your imagination. And think of how wonderful it will be to avoid the crowds by shopping by mail. Here is a whole new and exciting world of international salesmen waiting to tempt.

# Chapter 1

# THE STORY OF CHRISTMAS SYMBOLS

During the early days of Christianity, Christmas as we know it today did not exist. In fact, there is no absolutely certain proof that December 25 is even the actual date of the birth of Jesus Christ. No date is given in the Bible.

Early Christians considered the celebration of birthdays to be a pagan custom. They made no festival of even Christ's birthday. But, as time passed, people began to feel differently. They tried to determine the proper date of this event. After historical investigation, December 25 was decided to be a good approximation, and it was declared officially.

This was the time of year of the old Roman festival Saturnalia. It was a season of gay revelry because, after the days of the year had grown shorter and shorter, now at last they were becoming longer again. Many early races made this change of the year a festival of rejoicing because of the distant but certain approach of spring.

So the Church thought it wise to celebrate Christmas at this same time and so transform the pagan festival rather than try to abolish it. The ancient practices could be incorporated into Christianity and given Christian significance.

Naturally, the Roman emperors of the time objected to this attempt by the Church, and many Christians were persecuted and put to death for observing Christes Masse. This means Mass of Christ and is the English name for the day which the Church observes as the birth of Christ.

In the year 303, the Emperor Diocletian ordered churches to be burned where Christmas was being celebrated. But later Emperor Constantine recognized the new faith and allowed its festivals to be celebrated. Soon the celebration of Christmas became an established custom.

Northern people, too, had a celebration at the same time of year as Saturnalia. They honored the god Thor and called their festival Yule.

Many of the pagan customs of Saturnalia and Yule were incorporated into the observance of Christmas. Many of these customs have come down to us today commingled in the symbols of Christmas. Long forgotten are their pagan origins.

## GIFTS

One of the things we look upon as a joy at Christmas is the giving of gifts. Actually the giving of gifts of candles and green wreaths was practiced during Saturnalia. And at the Calends, a three-day Roman New Year's festival celebrated starting January 1, houses were adorned with lights and greenery, and presents called *strenae* were given to friends, children, and the poor. As time went on the gifts became more elaborate. Sweet things were given to ensure the sweetness of the coming year. Lamps were gifts to wish light and warmth. Money or gold or silver objects were a wish for increasing wealth.

The early Church frowned on gift giving as a pagan custom. But the people enjoyed it too much to abandon it, and so finally the Church accepted the idea and sanctioned it. Gift giving could commemorate the splendid gifts of the Magi to the infant Jesus. By the twelfth century gifts on Christmas Eve were becoming a custom.

## EVERGREENS

As we have seen, the use of evergreens for decoration was also originally a pagan custom. The Romans used them during Saturnalia. Evergreens were worshiped as a symbol of immortality. Because they were always green, they were thought to possess magical properties.

The early Church forbade the use of them, but here again the custom was too deeply rooted and the ban was ignored. Finally the Church accepted the use of evergreens for decoration.

# WREATH

The wreath was an early Roman and Greek symbol of victory and glory. It was also in popular use during Saturnalia. Soon it began to figure in Christianity. One story used in the preachings of early missionaries on Christ's sufferings tells it this way. When Christ was crowned with thorny holly branches, the berries, then white, changed to blood red. As a result of this legend, the use of holly wreaths at Christmas became popular. Soon a lighted candle was placed in the center of the wreath to remind people of the new Light of the World, Jesus, born on Christmas Day. And so the wreath, a pagan symbol of victory and glory, plus the candle to signify the Light of the World, fulfills the promise of the Old Testament reminding us that the Lord would come as the Light of the World to bring the promised days of glory.

# HOLLY, IVY, MISTLETOE

Holly, ivy, and mistletoe were favorite decorations in early times, and they still are popular. They were life symbols because they were evergreen and especially since they bear fruit in winter, unlike most plants. Ivy was considered feminine; holly masculine. Both were necessary in the house to ensure the blessings of good luck and fertility.

Holly was believed to have the power of protection from witches, thunder, and lightning. The Burning Bush, from which God spoke to Moses, was thought to be holly.

In ancient Scandinavia, mistletoe was held sacred. They thought it brought good luck, fertility, protection from witchcraft, and was an antidote to poison. It was a plant of peace, and during the Yule season enemies resolved their differences under branches of mistletoe as a symbol of fidelity to the promise of friendship. Yet it was never included in the Christmas decorations of the Church, as holly and ivy, because somehow mistletoe never quite lost its heathen character. But it was used extensively in many homes, just as it is today.

The English started the custom of kissing under the mistletoe. To this day, girls standing under it cannot refuse to be kissed.

## THE CHRISTMAS TREE

The lovely custom we know today of decorating and lighting ever-green trees at Christmas seems to have come originally from Ger-many. No one is quite sure how or when it began, but there are a number of legends to explain it.

One of these tells us that in the eighth century, St. Boniface came from England to convert the heathen Germans from their worship of Thor to Christianity. At the time, these tribes made human sacrifices to their God under the sacred "Thunder Oak." It is said that St. Boni-face cut down the sacred oak and found a young fir tree straight and green, top pointing to the stars, standing amid the fallen ruins of the old oak. The people were angry at his deed, but St. Boniface pointed out that there was no stain of blood on the fir tree. He told them it was an evergreen, symbolizing everlasting life, to replace the heathen tree. He called it a Christmas tree, dedicated to love and good deeds instead of to bloodshed. People were instructed to keep it in the home with love and laughter rather than go into the forest for shameful secret rites under the Thunder Oak.

Another story has it that the Christmas tree stems from two medieval religious symbols: the Paradise Tree and the Christmas Light.

In medieval times, miracle plays were performed in the churches or on rough platforms in the churchyards. They were called miracle plays because they depicted the miracles worked by Christ, and Bible stories. They were put on to instruct and to entertain the people. One play told the story of the creation. Adam and Eve were shown eating the forbidden fruit and being expelled from Paradise. The only stage decoration was a fir tree hung with bright, shiny red apples to rep-resent the forbidden tree. It became popularly known as the Paradise Tree.

Miracle plays were abandoned by the fifteenth century because they had become irreverent, but the observance of the feast day of Adam and Eve on December 24 continued, and people erected Paradise Trees in their homes. The Roman Church never officially recognized sainthood for Adam and Eve, but the Eastern churches did, and the custom of observing this feast day with the tree spread throughout Europe.

Another religious custom, the Christmas Light, symbolizing the birth of Christ as the Light of the World, was celebrated on December 24, Christmas Eve.

In various countries it was the custom to build a small pyramid-like frame, usually decorated with glass balls and tinsel and with a candle on the top.

Along about the sixteenth century, people in Germany began combining the two ideas. The fir tree was now decorated with tinsel and balls and cookies, and the apples were discarded. The change was now to remind them that it was no longer a tree of sin, but a tree to symbolize the religious significance of the "sweet fruit of Christ's salvation of mankind." The Star Candle of Bethlehem was replaced by the star on the top of the tree. The idea spread throughout Europe and was brought to America by German immigrants.

A later story of the origin of the Christmas tree tells us that Martin Luther was out one evening during the holiday season and was so impressed by the beauty of the landscape and starlit sky that he cut down a fir tree to bring some of the atmosphere home to his wife. Once inside he placed small lighted candles on the branches and explained to her that this would be a symbol of the beautiful Christmas sky. He called it the Christmas Tree.

The first English Christmas tree appeared in 1821 at a court party for children. Ordinary people did not adopt the idea for a number of years. They still hung a garland of greenery, shaped like a double-looped May garland which they decorated with candles, a ring of red apples, ornaments, and a bunch of mistletoe suspended from the center. It hung from the middle of the ceiling, and sometimes long ribbons were attached to it with small gifts tied to them. They called this the Kissing Bough.

And then, of course, it could be said that the custom of the tree adorned with lights to decorate the home was borrowed from the popular old Roman tradition during the season of Saturnalia and the Calends, which coincided with the newer celebration of Christmas.

## CHRISTMAS DINNER AND FESTIVITIES

What is more traditional than the turkey dinner at Christmas? But turkey, though traditional now, was not known in Europe before 1542. Even then it was served only as one of many festive dishes.

Ordinary families celebrated with goose or beef or Christmas pies of many ingredients. Of course, in the great houses and castles the table was laden with the rarer delicacies. In fact, the whole celebration had a ritual.

The celebration started with the lord of the manor inviting the people from the countryside to a Christmas celebration at his castle. The great dining room filled with guests to partake of the Christmas feast. The table was crowded with roast peacock with tail spread and beak gilded, swan, venison, bustard, goose, chicken, roast beef, mince pie, plum pudding, and every delicacy available.

## CEREMONY OF THE BOAR'S HEAD

After the guests were seated, a trumpet was sounded. And thus began the ceremony of the Boar's Head. Boar was an enemy to be reckoned with in medieval England. Dangerous travel by foot through thick forests with long, lonely stretches made people wary of the vicious boar. Therefore, the boar's head on a silver platter borne in procession to the table signified a victory over evil. And so the procession began. Into the room filed the pages, heralds, torch-bearers, trumpeter, then two minstrels carrying the trophy. They placed it with a flourish before the host at the head of the table, and then the guests and servants joined in singing the "Boar's Head Carol."

## WASSAIL

When they had finished eating, the Christmas drink was served from the wassail bowl. It was a mixture of hot ale, spices, sugar, eggs, and roasted apples floating on the top. Sometimes a thick cream was added and French bread or sippets of toast. A large cup was filled and then passed around the table. As each guest drank he cried, "Wes hal" or "Waes hael," meaning, "Be thou whole" or "To your health" or "Good luck." Today we say, "Wassail," the Anglo-Saxon for "Here's to your good health."

After the feast, the guests assembled in the great drawing room for the entertaining events to follow.

## YULE LOG

The ceremony started with the lighting of the Yule log by the lord of the castle. This event dates back to the time of the Saxons and Goths, who burned such a log at their festival of the winter solstice. A great Yule log which was often the whole trunk of a large tree was ceremoniously hauled in with the youngest member of the assembly riding astride as the Yule sprite. The log was lighted with a piece of wood carefully saved from last year's log. This was to ensure good fortune for the household during the coming year.

## THE LORD OF MISRULE

After the lighting, the castle gates were opened to admit the Weary Traveler, who begged for food and warmth, promising entertainment in return. He was taken to the hearth to tell the assemblage stories from many lands. This traveler did not appear by chance. He was selected at Halloween to play this part in the festival, and his performance was rewarded with cakes and ale. Once inside, he removed his ragged clothes and revealed himself as the Lord of Misrule for the holiday season. His job was to take charge of the revelries and to keep things lively and merry. He was what we would call today the Master of Ceremonies.

## HOODMAN-BLIND

The Lord of Misrule then called forth his companions, the mummers and jesters, and the fun began. First he placed a hood over the head of a guest and the rough-and-tumble game of hoodman-blind, popular during the fifteenth and sixteenth centuries, began. This was the origin of the game we know today as blindman's buff.

## SWORD DANCE

Next the young nobles from the countryside came forth to perform the traditional Sword Dance. The sword was a symbol of rank and authority, as it still is today.

## MORRIS DANCE

And then the Morris Men with tinkling bells and painted sticks performed the Morris Dance.

## MUMMERS' PLAY

The crowd was now ready for the play. The mummers came forth to perform the traditional Christmas play, always about St. George and the Dragon.

## THE WAITS

After the play came the time for singing by the Waits. These were originally minstrels of the court whose duty was to watch and call out the hours. Hence the name Waits. But by the sixteenth century the word came to mean a band of people who went from house to house singing Christmas carols. Eventually the Waits became known as carolers.

## PANTOMIME

When the singing was over, the children were called on to perform. Each year they put on a pantomime of Mother Goose rhymes. The name Mother Goose was supposed to have originated from Queen Goosefoot of the French legends, which were widely told by word of mouth for many years before being written down.

## COUNTRY DANCE

The final event of the Christmas ceremony was the Country Dance. Everybody joined in this event. Partners took the floor and the dancing began. A sixteenth-century country dance of much popularity was called "Sweet Kate," which was similar to a Virginia reel of today.

## CHRISTMAS CARDS

The idea of not having Christmas cards to send to loved ones and friends seems appalling. But the Christmas card is a relatively new event on the Christmas scene. An Englishman by the name of Sir Henry Cole commissioned the London artist John Calcott Horsely to create a card for him in the year 1843. Sir Henry was accustomed to writing personal notes to his many friends during the holiday season, and he found it to be more and more difficult a chore to keep up with. So he decided that a card of greeting might suit the occasion and relieve him of the task. Horsely designed a three-panel card in color. The two side panels illustrated the virtues of feeding the hungry and clothing the needy. The center panel showed the family at Christmas dinner. Beneath this scene was written, "A Merry Christmas and a Happy New Year to You." Christmas cards had been born, but they were not yet in wide use.

But in 1874 a German immigrant to the United States named Louis Prang decided to make Christmas cards to sell. He owned a small lithographing shop in Roxbury, Massachusetts, and he designed some colored floral cards which he offered for sale. Americans took to the idea, and Christmas cards gained a place among our Christmas traditions.

## THE CHRISTMAS SEAL

Most of us are familiar with the Christmas seal. This seal was the brain child of a Danish postal clerk named Einar Holboell. He felt strongly about the terrible toll taken by the disease tuberculosis. In 1903 he devised an idea to raise money to fight this illness. He designed the Christmas seal. It became popular and did indeed provide the much-needed funds.

Meanwhile Jacob Riis, a social worker in the United States, heard of the idea. Knowing how badly needed funds were for this cause in the United States, Mr. Riis promoted the Christmas seal idea here. He called his stamp the Christmas stamp. It has become a familiar part of our Christmas scene.

## POINSETTIA

Here in the United States we think of the poinsettia as a Christmas symbol. It is found pictured on Christmas cards, gift wrapping, and ribbon. Poinsettia plants are sold everywhere during the season. They help brighten our Christmas with their fiery scarlet color, creating their own brilliant display for the festival of light and fire. Their Mexican name is translated as "flower of the holy night." They were popularized in the United States and Canada in 1828 by Dr. Poinsett, thus the English name poinsettia.

It is easy to see that many symbols and many peoples of yesteryear as well as of recent years have influenced what today we consider our Christmas symbols. As each generation carries on with its particular Christmas traditions, there is a further blending of the ethnic past with an addition of new ideas which may someday become part of the established symbols of our Christmas celebration.

# Chapter 2

# EARLY CHRISTMAS CELEBRATIONS
# IN THE UNITED STATES

The Reformation in the sixteenth century brought sharp changes in the Christmas celebration. The sacrifice of the Mass was suppressed. The Holy Eucharist, the liturgy of the Divine Office, the sacramentals, and ceremonies disappeared. There were no more colorful processions, nor was there veneration of the blessed Virgin Mary and the saints. All this was ridiculed as superstition.

The sermon and prayer service on Christmas Day remained, although the people kept alive the feasting and good-natured reveling during Christmas.

The German Lutherans still celebrated the Christ Child in their churches and homes. But in England the Puritans condemned even the reduced religious celebration in the Anglican Church after the separation from Rome. They wished to abolish Christmas as a religious and popular feast. They felt that the Sabbath (Sunday) should be the first ranking institution. They published pamphlets denouncing Christmas as pagan and sinful. In Scotland punishment was inflicted on any person caught observing it.

When the Puritans in England came to political power, they outlawed Christmas. In 1642 church services and civic festivities on Christmas Day were forbidden. In 1644, December 25 was declared a day of fast and penance. But the people ignored this and continued to celebrate. By 1647, Parliament ordained that anyone celebrating would be punished. Town criers were sent through the streets days in advance of Christmas to warn people not to observe "the superstitious festival." Markets and stores were instructed to remain open on that day.

Riots broke out because people defied the law, and people were jailed, hurt, and some lost their lives. Anglican ministers who held services and decorated their churches were removed from their posts. Slowly the observance of Christmas died out, although many people celebrated in private.

In 1660, with the restoration of the monarchy, Christmas celebration returned, but no longer was there the deeply religious observance. Feasts and reveling now ruled the day.

But the Pilgrims and Puritans escaping from England to America did not believe in festivals. They thought that merrymaking was for heathens. They would not celebrate Christmas Day. On that day it was decreed that people should work even harder. If anyone was caught celebrating the occasion, he was fined.

In fact, in New England there was no Christmas celebration for many years. Until the late nineteenth century Christmas celebration was outlawed.

In Boston those who refused to report to work on Christmas were often fired. As late as 1870, Boston public schools were open on Christmas Day. Any pupil who stayed home to observe Christmas was punished, sometimes by public dismissal.

When the German immigrants came to this country with their Christmas tree, and the Irish with their custom of lights in the window, and both with the idea of the crèche, and carols, hymns, church services and abstaining from work on December 25, their neighbors began to join in the customs because they seemed so charming.

When the people in New England finally began celebrating Christmas again, it was not considered as big a holiday as Thanksgiving. In some smaller villages a large Christmas tree was set up in the town hall for everyone. Parents hung gifts for their children on these branches rather than on a tree at home. The tree was not decorated as it is now, and when the gifts were given out the tree remained bare. After the gift giving there was usually entertainment consisting of recitations, songs, and a speech.

By the late nineteenth century Christmas was being celebrated in the United States. There was a turkey dinner with cranberry sauce, candy, plum pudding, and pie. Church bells chimed and carolers sang on Christmas Eve and early on Christmas morning. Stockings were hung in a row by the fireplace, and children waited for Santa Claus and the gifts he would bring.

In the South skyrockets were set off, cannons roared, horns were tooted, and bells rang. Brass bands played songs like "My Maryland" and "Dixie," and soldiers marched. The houses were decorated with greens, and mistletoe was hung above the doorways.

Parts of Spanish New Mexico started their celebrations a week before Christmas Day. In the evenings people went in groups from door to door acting out the Bible story of Mary and Joseph seeking lodging. Afterwards they held parties to celebrate. And on Christmas Eve people gathered together to put on a Christmas play about the story of Bethlehem.

The Shakers observed Christmas by allowing the men and women to sit at the table together. During the rest of the year they ate at separate tables. The dinner was eaten in silence. Afterwards the people rose in their places and sang, marking time with their hands and feet. Then they swayed their bodies from side to side in the manner that had given this sect its name of Shakers. After the singing the elder chanted a prayer, and then the people filed out of the building in silence.

Pennsylvania Dutch children celebrated by looking out for Pelznickel (Santa Claus). Someone impersonated him on Christmas Eve by dressing up as an old man with a long white beard. He carried a switch and a bag of toys. He went from house to house asking parents if the children were good. Good ones received a gift. Bad ones got tapped with the switch.

Puerto Rican children during this time were told that Santa flew through the air like a bird. They made boxes to place on the roof or in the courtyard for Santa to drop the gifts into.

And in Alaska a popular Christmas custom of those belonging to the Greek Church was "going around with the star." People went from house to house in a line behind one person who carried a large, brightly colored paper star. The followers all carried lanterns on long poles. They sang carols at each place they stopped, and people gave them refreshments for their efforts.

While in Hawaii the natives said that Santa came to the islands by boat.

Today, of course, Christmas celebrations are widespread and very similar throughout the United States. Books, magazines, television, and the mobility of the population acquaint all of us with each other's customs. More and more we are adopting bits and parts of other cultures' Christmas celebrations into our own, making the occasion more truly international in flavor.

# Chapter 3

# THE CHRISTMAS TREE
# IN MANY COUNTRIES

Here in the United States we think of the Christmas tree as an evergreen decked with colorful Christmas balls, tinsel, perhaps roping and tiny figures of angels or Santa. But in other countries of the world the tree may take on a very different look. Or perhaps instead of the tree there is a crèche.

## AUSTRIA

The Austrian tree is a magnificent sight, colorful and with a storybook quality. It is decorated with *Kripps,* which are carved-out fruits filled with tiny scenes of the Nativity. There are madonna and child, golden angels, etc. Added to these charming hangings are Christmas balls magnificently decorated with pictures, miniature horns, colorful roping around the tree branches, and an over-all covering of artificial snow.

Often an outdoor tree is dressed for the birds at Christmas to supply them with food through the cold winter. Orange baskets are filled with raisins and suet, popcorn balls and string, seeds, doughnuts, apples, and a bread star studded with cranberries are on the tree.

## BELGIUM

Belgian trees feature gingerbread men and the white-bearded, red-dressed figure of the German Father Thor. The bells, horns, and drums on the tree date back to pagan days when they were used to frighten away evil spirits during solstice rites. Stars, clowns, and clusters of nuts are added to make this a bright, colorful sight and show the gaiety of the Christmas season.

## CZECHOSLOVAKIA

Eggshell ornaments decorated in pretty colors or to look like strange fish are the Czech specialty, as well as many representations of the angels who accompanied St. Nicholas. Gaily colored pinwheels looking like falling snowflakes or twinkling stars are suspended by thread. Gilded walnuts and many varieties of bells are hung in clusters on bright ribbon to create an interesting tree. A small crèche is often placed at the base of the tree.

## DENMARK

Danish trees feature mobiles. Paper bells, stars, snowflakes, and hearts are hung in eye-catching mobiles. Woven paper baskets, paper cutouts of Jul-Nisse, paper-covered red drums, and toy soldiers of wood are popular decorations as well as stringing of miniature Danish flags which are draped among the tree branches.

## ENGLAND

The Christmas tree came to England in 1841, when Prince Albert, of Saxe-Coburg, Germany, set up a tree in Windsor Castle for his wife, Queen Victoria. At first the decorations were in the German tradition, but soon English customs arose. One of these customs was the use of Christmas cards being hung from the tree as decorations. Candy and sugar plums tucked into cornucopias, silver-filigree baskets, tiny gift packages wrapped in brocade and velvet with colorful satin ribbons, red-golden swags, and a gossamer angel on top of the tree and tiny candles set among the branches typified the English tree.

## FINLAND

Father Christmas is traditionally prominent on Finnish Christmas trees. His white-bearded face and red stocking cap hang gaily along with baskets of beauty (cornucopias with simply designed sides and a colorful pompon on the top of the cone), golden paper or colored pipe-cleaner birds, garlands of tinsel, large pine cones, and ropes of miniature Finnish flags.

## FRANCE

The French usually have a crèche rather than a Christmas tree. Evergreens are not readily available and are expensive to import. The manger scene is set on the mantel or prominently on a table, and greenery can be added to heighten the setting effect.

## GERMANY

The Thuringian mountain region of Germany supplied Christmas ornaments for most of us in the United States for many years. Whole families in this area worked year round preparing the decorations for the seasonal trade. Until World War II they were the chief suppliers of such ornaments. During the war the scarcity of decorations prompted American production of such items. And after the war Japan became a leading producer of them.

The German tree features the bearded face and peaked cap of Father Thor, representations of St. Nicholas as a bishop, and Kriss Kringle, the golden-haired angel. There are hanging apples and oranges originally from the miracle plays of medieval days when the evergreen tree, representing the Paradise Tree, was hung with "forbidden fruit," symbolizing the temptation of Adam and Eve in the Garden of Eden. Ball ornaments represent the bags of gold of St. Nicholas. Hand-carved birds and animals from the worship scene at Bethlehem, white doves and paper stars, angels and tiny horns representing the heralds of Christ's birth, and clusters of bells as well as gingerbread men and houses are in the traditional style.

## HOLLAND

The tree in Holland has its branches decked with sugar bells, *Kerstkransjes*, which are wreath-like cookies that the children are allowed to pull off to eat, and chocolate cookies in the form of St.

Nicholas. Small candles are set among the tree branches, and tiny apples and Christmas balls add to the color of the tree.

## HUNGARY

Agricultural magic figures greatly in Hungarian Christmas lore. The tree, naturally, has agricultural accents. Nuts, cookies, Christmas fudge called *Szalon Cukor* in cornucopias, popcorn strings, and other edibles trim the tree. Christmas cards with messages of good fortune are added for decoration.

## IRELAND

The Irish never really adopted the Christmas tree, and so the manger scene is the center of interest in Irish homes at Christmas. And because the English attempted to suppress the religious beliefs of the Irish, the priests were forced to conceal their identities, and another custom came into being at Christmas. The Irish placed a light in the window so the priests could find their way and know they were welcome to visit the farmhouses and homes to conduct religious services in secret. The English were told the light was just a Christmas custom of no special significance.

The Irish brought the light-in-the-window custom to the United States when they came, and it was adopted by many Americans who thought it was charming. Thus it became part of our Christmas custom.

## ITALY

Each Italian home has its *praesepio,* or manger scene, rather than a Christmas tree. The figures are often hand-carved and minute in detail of features and dress.

The scene is often set out in the shape of a triangle and furnishes the base of a pyramid-like structure called the *ceppo*. This is a light wooden framework arranged to make a pyramid several feet high. Several tiers of cardboard or thin shelves are supported by this framework. It is entirely decorated with colored paper, gilt pine cones, and miniature colored pennants. Small candles are fastened to the tapering sides. A star or small doll is suspended at the apex of the triangular sides. The shelves above the crib scene hold small gifts of fruit, candy, and presents.

The *ceppo* is in the old Tree of Light tradition, which became the Christmas tree in other countries.

Many homes feature a *ceppo* for each child in the family.

## JAPAN

Christmas was not widely celebrated in Japan until the beginning of the twentieth century. Japanese became acquainted with the holiday because of the products made for Christmas celebrations around the world which were being produced in Japan.

Many Japanese now have trees at Christmas as a secular holiday devoted to the love of children. The tree is decked with small toys, dolls, paper ornaments, gold paper fans and lanterns, wind chimes, and miniature candles set among the tree branches to create a pretty tree.

## LITHUANIA

Tree ornaments are made of wheat or rye straw for the Lithuanian Christmas tree. The women gather it and fashion it artistically in many designs. Some are made of varied lengths of straw strung together by needle and thread to form bird cages, stars, bell towers, and hundreds of geometric designs. Birds are created of milkweed pods or with eggshell bodies and paper or feather wings. Straw is also cut into small pieces and glued on traditional folk designs drawn on paper. Reproductions of the wayside shrines found on country roads are made of straw. Even figures of straw are created to hang on the tree.

Straw, of course, is a reminder in this small agricultural country of the past harvest and the wish for abundant crops in the year to come.

The Christmas Elf, who brings the gifts to Lithuanian children, sways inside a teardrop made of straw. He decorates the tree very colorfully. And tiny angels hang beneath sheaves of wheat, with touches of red yarn on their robes. Straw crosses backed with red felt and straw garlands cascading from the whisk-broom angel perched high on the top of the tree make a charming display.

## MEXICO

Traditionally Christmas is celebrated with a representation of the Nativity scene called the *pesebra*.

Plate I shows a stylized Mexican Christmas tree which might be used in conjunction with the Nativity scene. It illustrates how liberty can be taken with a traditional tree form to create a more individualized decoration, as in this tree designed for Herb Alpert by Hallmark Galleries.

The tree is made of wrought iron and tin. It is an enlargement of a typical eighteen-inch-high Mexican ornament used at Christmas. It is ordinarily sold in Mexican markets at Christmas time and is found set beside a Mexican market scene with various folk art objects surrounding it.

The same plate illustrates how a Christmas tree can be designed to reflect your hobby. Julia Child, TV's French Chef, has designed a Christmas tree of stainless steel. It features cooking implements such as molds, whips, frying pans, saucepans, foods, and bottles of liquor which she uses in French cooking.

Try creating a tree featuring your hobby if you are looking for something new in your Christmas display.

## NORWAY

The tip of the Norwegian Christmas tree is traditionally decorated by placing three candles, representing the Three Wise Men, on it. *Jule-nissen,* the invisible, troublemaking, mischief-loving elf-like creatures who make thumping noises in the attic, overturn the milk, sour the cream, and cause countless mishaps in homes with small children, feature prominently on the tree. They are dressed in red with pointed caps and long white whiskers. They ride on *Jule-buken* (goats) which bump bad children.

## POLAND

Tree ornaments differ in Polish cities from countryside decorations. But stars of many varieties feature prominently in both. Intricate paper designs in red and white (the national colors) are popular. Many varieties of birds, peacock, porcupine, the royal crest, bright shields, heart-shaped ornaments, garlands, and angels are greatly used.

## RUSSIA

During czarist Russia days ornate Christmas balls and brilliant glass prisms, as well as icon-like images of the Virgin Mary and saints, decorated the Christmas tree along with birds, animals, nuts, and candy.

## SCOTLAND

Christmas cards, tinsel, garlands, miniature stockings, Christmas balls, bells, and stars decorate the Scottish tree on Christmas.

## SPAIN

Spanish homes celebrate Christmas around the crib or *nacimiento,* where elaborate crèche figures are displayed.

## SWEDEN

Wooden ornaments in the form of Tompte the Elf, angels, straw baskets filled with nuts, and the hand-dipped white candles balanced by apples (the traditional apple sticks) hung below decorate the Swedish Christmas tree. *Jul-docka,* which are straw dolls in the form of children and animals, are also favorite tree as well as table decorations at Christmas time.

Sometimes a stylized wooden tree is used as the Christmas tree. Each branch has an apple hung at the end, and the top of the tree is decorated with a spray of golden wheat tied with a ribbon. *Pepparkakor* (very thin crisp ginger cookies cut in fancy holiday shapes— star, bells, horses, children, etc.—and decorated with white frosting) are hung on the branches of the tree. (See cookie recipes.)

## SWITZERLAND

White garlands and snow-white birds, candy baskets, bells, sleighs, oranges, and stars enhance the Swiss Christmas tree.

## UKRAINE

The Ukrainian Christmas tree features a spider and a web. It is considered lucky to find a spider web in the house on Christmas because of an old Ukrainian legend. It is said that a poor woman who could not provide any trimmings for her children's Christmas tree was surprised to find on Christmas morning that spiders had covered the tree with their webs during the night. When the Christmas morning sun struck the tree, the webs turned to silver. So unexpected fortune is associated with finding a spider's web on Christmas. The artificial spider and web decorating the tree are to ensure good fortune. Colorful garlands and geometric designs made of straw are also used to dress the tree.

## UNITED STATES

The American tree is, of course, a conglomerate of the many cultures of Europe. We have borrowed the tree itself from the German troops that brought it with them when they came to fight in the Revolutionary War.

In early days decorations were homemade and simple. Apples, oranges, nuts, popcorn balls, cranberry strings, and paper ornaments were used. Later on German decorations were imported and trees took on a grander look.

But Americans did contribute their own ideas to the decorations. Thomas Edison gave us electric lights, which are used in profusion on our trees as well as on trees of other countries. Outdoor tree lights are another American innovation. A community Christmas tree, as well as individual home decorations, and spraying trees in various colors are still more American ideas.

American trees feature Christmas balls, bells, horns, Santa Claus dolls, elf dolls, garlands, tinsel, colored lights, stars, angels, and bits and pieces of just about every Christmas tree in other lands. The crèche is used widely but usually in conjunction with the tree. New decorating ideas are born each year, and the American tree has a bit of the old and a bit of the new. Something for everyone.

## YUGOSLAVIA

The Yugoslavian tree features many angels in its decoration. Delicate web-like baskets, paper chains, tissue paper garlands, and colorful paper birds add to the charm of this tree.

# Chapter 4

# SANTA IN OTHER COUNTRIES

In most European countries the child Jesus was pictured as the gift bringer. He was thought to come with angels during the night to trim the tree and place presents beneath it.

But in Spanish-speaking countries, though the child Jesus brought the gifts, there was no tree. Instead, the crib and manger were set up to remain empty for nine days. On Christmas morning a picture of the Holy Child was found in the crib and the gifts arranged in front of the crib.

After the Reformation, the feast of St. Nicholas was abolished and people forgot him and his religious significance. Instead, they substituted the Christmas Man for the saint.

The Dutch, however, made their Christmas Man a Nordic figure in bishop's garments. He came on a white charger on Christmas Eve. When the carillons rang, the fireplaces and window sills were decorated with children's wooden shoes stuffed with hay and carrots and a dish of water set alongside to provide refreshments for Sinter Klaas's white horse. He was thought to ride through the streets with his little Moorish servant, Black Piet. When he stopped by, the hay was replaced with nuts, apples, candy, and gifts. And on Christmas Eve good children still find "chocolate lover dolls" at their places on the supper table.

When the Dutch came to America, they brought Sinter Klaas with them. The name became Anglicized to Santa Claus, and he was changed from a bishop to a jolly old man. The English added their version of Father Christmas to him as well. Now he delivered gifts on Christmas and placed them in stockings rather than in wooden shoes.

Santa's home and factory became the North Pole (as in the German Father Thor legend), and the sleigh and reindeer and custom of sliding down the chimney were added to make our present-day Santa Claus. Now he is a fairy-tale rather than a religious figure.

The idea of writing to Santa Claus requesting the gifts desired for Christmas stems from an old Advent custom. Advent is the time for prayer and fasting in preparation for Christmas. It was customary for children to write letters to the saint at this time, listing what they would like for Christmas.

## AUSTRIA

In Austria children put notes to "dear child Jesus in Heaven" on the window sill for St. Nicholas to take so that the Christ Child could bring the requested gifts on Christmas Eve. It is the custom for Nikkolo and the Krampus (the devil) to visit families with children on Christmas. Krampus is dressed in black with horns and a long red tongue. He carries chains and a bundle of birch branches to whack bad children. The good St. Nikkolo in miter, with his crosier, is dressed in white, gold, and red. He gives gifts to good children.

## BELGIUM

Belgian children place shoes, baskets, or dishes under the tree for St. Nicholas to fill on Christmas Eve. They put water, hay, and carrots outside the door to attract his gray horse to their home. St. Nicholas wears a bishop's robe and a miter, and he carries a pastoral staff. On Christmas morning the children find chairs tipped over in their rooms and further disarray to show evidence that St. Nicholas has been there. Good children find their shoes filled with gifts. Bad ones find switches stuffed in theirs.

## CZECHOSLOVAKIA

In Czechoslovakia, St. Nicholas descends from heaven on a golden cord accompanied by an angel in white and a devil called Cert, dressed in black. Cert carries a whip and chains to beat bad children. The angel leaves gifts for the good children.

# FINLAND

Father Christmas brings children their gifts in Finland. In some sections he is known as Wainamoinen or Ukko. He is an old man with a long white mustache. He wears a white peaked cap with blue trim and a red coat.

# FRANCE

Today French children place their *sabots* (shoes), not stockings, near the crèche to have them filled with candy by Petit Noël (the Christ Child), who comes down the chimney. He does not bring their gifts on Christmas Day, but on New Year's Day instead. But in the old days children received their gifts from Le Père Noël (Father Christmas), who came with Le Père Fouettard (Father Spanker), whose duty it was to reward bad children with a spanking while small token gifts were left in the *sabots* by Le Père Noël for the good children.

# GERMANY

The first Santa Claus in Germany was patterned after the god Thor, who became Father Thor or Father Christmas in early Germany. He was an old man with a long white beard who was friendly to the people. He roared through the heavens in the thunder of a rainstorm in a golden chariot drawn by two white goats, Cracker and Gnasher. Lightning was his power, and his color was red. He lived in the far north among ice and snow, and he fought the gods of ice and snow to help the people conquer the dreaded winter. He became the first Father Christmas and brought gifts to the children as part of his benevolence to the people.

When Christianity arose in Germany, the figure of St. Nicholas, a fourth-century bishop of Myra, in Asia Minor, captured the imagination of the people. He was known for his miracles and generosity. He became the patron saint of children by, according to the legend, restoring to life three boys who had been killed. He became the Santa Claus figure in Germany, and the feast of St. Nicholas was celebrated on December 6. He was represented as a tall, thin fellow with a peaked hat, riding a white horse and accompanied by his servant, Rupprecht, a thin, dark man carrying a sack to put bad children into. St. Nicholas, of course, carried gifts for the good children.

When Martin Luther began his teachings and a large part of Germany separated from the Roman Catholic Church, Kriss Kringle replaced St. Nicholas in the folklore. She was a young girl wearing a golden crown and carrying a small Christmas tree, "the tree of light." She was considered a messenger from the Christ Child and personified the idea of gift giving.

## HUNGARY

The Hungarian children believe that a male Kriss Kringle brings their gifts. He is dressed in white and rides a white horse.

## ITALY

Italian children hang up their stockings on the Feast of the Epiphany, January 6. They commemorate the visit of the Three Kings to Bethlehem. They are expecting Befana, a kind of female Santa Claus. She is a witch-like character who rides around on a broom. Supposedly the Three Wise Men stopped at her hut to ask directions on their way to Bethlehem and asked her to join them. She declined. She was too busy. Later a shepherd asked her to go pay her respects to the Infant Jesus, and again she said no. Later when it was dark and she saw a great light in the heavens she thought perhaps she should have gone with the Wise Men. She gathered some toys belonging to her own baby, who had died, and ran to find the kings and the shepherd. But Befana could not find them or the stable. Each year she looks again for the Christ Child. And each year she cannot find him and leaves the gifts for the children of Italy.

## LITHUANIA

Lithuanian children receive their gifts from the Christmas Elf.

## MEXICO

In Mexico, Santa is not as popular as the figure of Quetzalcoatl, the Aztec god of the sun. He is an old man with a long white beard and flowing white robes. Before Christmas children write letters to the Christ Child listing what they want. And on the eve of Epiphany, January 6, they place their shoes at the foot of their beds for the Three Magi to fill.

## PHILIPPINE ISLANDS

On Christmas Eve shoes are put in the window by the children in the Philippine Islands. They expect the Three Kings to fill them.

## POLAND

Before Christmas children in Poland write letters telling what they wish to receive and place them on the window sill for the Wise Men. Then on Christmas Eve, after supper, the children are examined on their knowledge of religion by the Star Man (the village priest). If they do well, they receive small gifts from the Wise Men. The Wise Men are impersonated by three young men who carry a star and sing carols. Gifts are believed to come from the stars, and the Wise Men act as the emissaries.

## RUSSIA

In Russia it was Baboushka who brought gifts to the good girls and boys. She was a witch-like person who had misdirected the Wise Men on their way to Bethlehem. Because of this she had forever to journey throughout the land knocking on each door with her staff, seeking the Infant Child. While the children were asleep, she entered with a candle to look at them and then slip a toy under the pillow.

## SOUTH AMERICA

South American children leave notes to "Little Jesus" during Posada. They leave them in front of the crib for the angels to take to heaven for answering.

## SPAIN

On the eve of Epiphany, Spanish children fill their shoes with straw for the camels of the Three Kings. It is thought that each year the Wise Men repeat their journey to Bethlehem and pass through Spain on the way. As they pass by, the camels eat the straw and the shoes are filled with gifts by Balthasar, who rides on a donkey.

In the early days stockings were hung up by young girls on St. Nicholas eve, December 6, because of a belief that St. Nicholas would provide dowries for poor girls. He supposedly threw three purses of gold into a poor man's home to provide dowries for his three daughters. So in some places girls hung long, stocking-shaped purses at their doors. But after a while they began to hang their stockings on Christmas Eve instead of on December 6, and it soon became a Christmas custom.

## SWEDEN

Jul-nisen in his red robe, pointed cap, and long white beard, riding his goat, brings Christmas gifts to good Swedish children.

## SWITZERLAND

The tradition of St. Nicholas is observed in most parts of Switzerland. He arrives on December 6 and distributes fruit, candy, and toys. Sometimes there is a parade in his honor. A giant figure of St. Nicholas leads a group of children dressed in long white nightgowns and masks. The paraders blow long Swiss horns and ring bells. They solicit toys and fruit as they march, and later distribute the gifts among themselves.

In some regions Samichlaus is eagerly awaited on the eve of December 5. He wears a red laughing mask, a flowing white beard, fur-trimmed robes, and he carries a staff to support him and a large, well-stuffed sack of gifts. He proceeds from the village church distributing gifts on the way. Boys wearing high-peaked snow hoods and robes and carrying a cross and banners, along with the church choir and clergy, sing Christmas songs as they precede him along the way.

Other villages await Father Christmas and his wife, Lucy, the gift bringers who visit the children. Lucy comes from the Scandinavian tradition of St. Lucy's feast day, December 13. Father Christmas is a jovial red-faced man who has a white beard and wears a fur-trimmed robe. He brings gifts for boys. Lucy wears a round white cap over her braids and is dressed in a silk gown with a laced bodice. She brings presents for the girls.

In still other parts of Switzerland the Christ Child is awaited. He travels across the land in a large, gift-filled sleigh drawn by six reindeer, much as the American Santa does. He distributes toys, candy, and fancy-shaped Christmas cookies to good children.

# Chapter 5

# CUSTOMS, LEGENDS, AND SUPERSTITIONS ASSOCIATED WITH CHRISTMAS

Throughout the years many superstitions, legends, and customs have become associated with Christmas. Decorations, food specialties, and ceremonies grew up in each country representing its people's ideas of how the holiday should be celebrated.

## ARMENIA

Christmas customs are primarily religious in Armenia. The week before Christmas is one of strict fasting, which ends after the Christmas Eve Communion.

When the family returns home after Communion, the house is lit with candles and the evening meal is served. After dinner the children go caroling in groups and are rewarded with cookies, fruit, candy, and small coins for their efforts.

Young men give their sweethearts special gifts at this time. Included, by custom, are twelve pieces of cake, one for each month, also a candle, some eggs, raisins, and sweetmeats, and some perfumed cosmetics. This is to prove that he can provide her with the necessities and the luxuries of life.

Christmas morning church services are held again, and water is blessed for use throughout the Christmas season for purification. At home it is mixed with earth and kept in a special bowl. It is used only for symbolic cleansing of dishes and other household items.

The next three days are for visiting neighbors and friends, and the third day is especially set aside for the women to visit each other. New Year's Day is the time for all to visit the priest. Men and women go in separate groups. They wish him well and receive a special blessing and a piece of cake.

Newly married bridegrooms visit their in-laws at this time. A money gift is given to the mother-in-law by the groom. She gives him some clothing in return.

Round, thick cakes of a special dough with raisins and almonds are made for New Year's visiting. A coin is baked into one piece. The finder of the coin will have good luck in the coming year.

## BULGARIA

Before breakfast the man of the house sprinkles some corn from a stocking onto the doorstep saying, "Christ is born." The others in the household reply, "He is born indeed." Then the man makes a series of wishes.

He goes to the fireplace and strikes sparks from the Yule log. At each blow he wishes good health to the horses, the cattle, the goats, and all the livestock. He ends by wishing for a good harvest.

The ashes are collected from the fire, and a coin is hidden in them. The Yule log is not burned completely, but pieces of the burned ends are placed in fruit trees to ensure a good crop for the year.

## CZECHOSLOVAKIA

There is caroling in the streets and in the homes on Christmas and dancing and eating after the fasting period, which ends on Christmas Eve with a special dinner. Christmas is a time for visiting, and it is customary for those who have quarreled during the year to forgive each other publicly.

Carolers go from house to house carrying miniature Bethlehem scenes and giving informal concerts. It is customary to invite them in for a glass of wine and *vanocka,* a sweet roll filled with almonds and raisins. Little boys dressed up as the Three Kings also go about singing for treats.

A very great blessing was thought to be received if the children slept on a bedding of straw and hay on the floor under the Christmas table on Christmas Eve to allow them to take part in the grace and privilege of the Lord's poor and humble birth.

Christmas is also a time of fortunetelling and forecasting the future. Girls float little boats made of half of a walnut shell in a tub of water with lit candles in them. It is said that the girl whose candle burns longest will marry during the coming year.

The girls also draw sticks from a pile of kindling wood. A long stick drawn means a tall husband, a thick stick indicates a stout husband, and so on.

Melted lead is dropped into a pan of water, and the shape the lead takes as it cools is used to forecast one's future husband's occupation.

Tiny candles are also lighted, placed in walnut shells, and set afloat in a large bowl of water by members of the family. Each watches his own boat to see if he will have smooth sailing during the coming year.

And a branch of a cherry tree is broken off at the beginning of Advent and placed in a pot of water in the kitchen to keep it in warm air. The twig usually bursts into bloom at Christmas time to make a festive house decoration. But of greater importance, the flowering is considered an omen of good luck. The girl who tended it will find a good husband within the year if the branch bloomed exactly on Christmas Eve.

## DENMARK

The house is decorated with holly and mistletoe and decked with Danish flags, and the family goes to church for the Christmas service. When they return they have a feast of roast goose with apple and prune stuffing, red cabbage, white potatoes, doughnuts, cookies, and *grot*.

*Grot* is a rich rice pudding covered with sugar and sprinkled with cinnamon. A hole is scooped out of the center and is filled with butter. One almond is put into the pudding. Whoever gets the almond in his portion of *grot* has to make a speech and receives a gift.

The Danes include their animals in the festivities, too. Barn animals and pets receive extra rations at Christmas, and food is put outdoors for the birds.

# ENGLAND

Though we think of the English Christmas dinner in terms of boar's head and roasted peacock as in the traditional pictures, in reality roast beef and plum pudding are now the traditional English Christmas meal.

On Devember 26, the Feast of St. Stephen, the English celebrate Boxing Day. In medieval days the priests emptied the alms boxes of their churches on this day to distribute gifts to the poor. Servants and workers also kept "boxes" for their savings and put Christmas gift money received from their employers into it. The day after Christmas they would break the boxes open to count the money. It was also the first workday after Christmas, the day on which tenants received their Christmas gift boxes from the landowners. And so the custom of giving and accepting gifts (boxes) gave the day its name.

Even today the Yule log is a tradition in England. Many northern farmers still consider it bad luck if the customary Yule log burns out. And if a cross-eyed person or a barefooted person enters the house while the log is burning, it is considered an ill-omen. And a charred stick from the Yule log is still placed under the bed to keep lightning from striking the house.

# FINLAND

At Christmas the Finnish house receives a thorough cleaning and washing. And on Christmas Eve the entire family takes the traditional sauna. This is a steaming rather than the usual bath. The Finnish bathhouse is a special separate building with three rooms in it. Red-hot stones are placed in one room, and then water is poured over them to fill the room with steam. The second room is for rubbing. A small switch of birch twigs is used to strike the body and so increase circulation. After leaving this room the bather takes a roll in the snow for further stimulation. Then he retires to the third room to dress.

After the sauna a light meal of barley porridge and almonds, with sugar and cream, fish, and prune tarts, is eaten. Superstition has it that if a vision is seen during this meal that person will marry during the coming year. It is also said that if one looks out of the window at this time someone will die during the coming year.

The dining-room table has a light wooden framework suspended from the ceiling above it. It is covered with straw to symbolize the stable where Christ was born. Paper stars are hung from it. Lamp lights from the room reflecting on it suggest the night sky.

After supper men used to hold wrestling matches on a straw-covered floor. Later the children would sleep on the straw in imitation of the Christ Child. Women would blacken their faces, dress in men's clothes, and visit their neighbors. No one spoke during this occasion, nor would anyone eat. It was a commemoration of the Moorish Wise Man.

On Christmas Day horse-drawn sleighs with many bells on them carried the families to church. Candles were placed in the windows of the houses on this day. After church the Christmas meal was eaten. Roast suckling pig with lingonberry relish or ham was a favorite. Dessert was rice pudding with one almond in it. The person who got the almond in his portion could expect good luck during the coming year.

## FRANCE

Celebration begins in France with the midnight Mass on Christmas Eve. It is followed by the traditional supper, Réveillon. Oysters, sausages, and wine used to be the special foods served, but baked ham, roast fowl, salads, fruit, bonbons, and pastries have been added to the meal. Christ cakes are baked and adorned with a figure made of sugar of the Holy Child. And in South France a Christmas loaf (*pain calendeau*) is quartered crosswise. It is eaten only after the first quarter is given to a poor person.

Restaurants and sidewalk cafés in the city are open all night serving Réveillon. The word is related to the military word reveille, from *réveiller,* to wake up, or first call of the day. And so Réveillon is said to be a symbolic spiritual awakening to the meaning of Christ's birth.

It used to be the custom to parade a large wicker figure of Melchior, one of the Three Kings, from door to door. He was strapped to a donkey's back with empty food hampers which would then be filled at the homes he passed. Later the food collected was distributed at the church to the poor.

The French also observed the Yule log tradition. In rural areas the entire family went out to select a tree. The father and eldest son then cut it down. Male members of the family, ranging by age along its length, carried the tree into the room. They circled the room three times, then placed the log in the fireplace. A glass of wine was poured over it, and the family sang a Christmas song.

In some provinces of France, a girl of marriageable age in the family would sit on the log, and a toast to her prospects was drunk by family and friends.

Sometimes the children were allowed to pull the log out of the fire once it was well ablaze and to beat it with sticks. The resulting sparks symbolized the departure of evil spirits, a residue of heathen rites.

The heat of the Yule log was used to prepare Réveillon. Even its ashes were used. They were sprinkled at the bases of fruit trees to ensure a good yield in the coming season. Yule log charcoal was saved too and used as a remedy for certain ailments of humans and animals.

In French cities where fireplaces and Yule logs were scarce, special cakes shaped like logs were baked and covered with chocolate icing to simulate the look of tree bark.

Another charming French custom was for the tradesmen to leave gifts for their customers on New Year's Day. The milkmen would leave cream. The grocer would send some fruit. And on Twelfth Night the baker would send a special flat cake of flaky pastry, *galette*. A tiny doll, a china *sabot,* or a bean was baked into it for luck. The one who found the charm was recognized as king or queen of the evening. Each tradesman expected a Christmas box from the customer in return for his gift.

In the French countryside the children prepared soft bedding in the manger with wisps of straw as tokens of prayers and good works. Each night the child would add one wisp for a virtue performed or an act of devotion, so supplying a soft straw bed to keep Him warm and comfortable.

# GERMANY

A great deal of Christmas tradition is Germanic in origin. That is to say, from the Germanic tribes who populated the heartland of Central Europe. Pagan customs intermingled with Christian practice when Christianity came to this area. The very word Yule came from the pagan custom of celebrating the winter solstice, which marked the end of the shortening hours of daylight and the sun's return to earth.

Evergreens decorated the homes, and large altars of flat stones were erected for the burning of fir boughs. It was believed that the goddess of the home, Hertha, descended through the smoke. Priests would forecast the future of those assembled at this time. Everyone took a lit twig of the sacred fire to kindle a Yule log on his own hearth. The log had to burn completely or misfortune would follow. Thus these mythological conceptions and the customs of the solstice, burning the Yule log and fortunetelling, became the foundations for the Christmas traditions of Europe.

Even today, German Christmas customs are colorful. In Bavaria, between St. Nicholas Day and Christmas, fairs (*Doms*) are held and one can buy toys, cookies, gingerbread men, and many other goodies at the booths. In other areas there are snow sculpture competitions.

The *Tannenbaum* (Christmas tree) is traditionally decorated in secret by the mother. It is lighted and revealed on Christmas Eve with nuts, cookies, and gifts to be found under its branches. And New Year's cards picture pots of cloves, marzipan, suckling pigs, and chimney sweeps as good luck symbols.

The whole family attends church on Christmas Eve in a colorful ceremony where the church is lighted by candles held by the worshipers.

## GREECE

A special loaf of bread with a cross marked on top and a coin baked inside is made for Christmas in Greece. Incense is burned in the house, and when the family gathers at the table for the evening meal, the bread is broken into small pieces by the parents.

The first piece is set aside for St. Basil, patriarch of Eastern monks, or for the Holy Virgin, or for the family's patron saint, whose icon is kept in the house.

The second piece is for the house, to bless the occupants. The third piece is for the farm animals, to bless them. The fourth piece symbolizes material possessions.

The remainder of the Christmas loaf is divided among family members, the oldest getting his first. As each receives his share, it is dipped in wine and eaten after saying, "This is in remembrance of St. Basil, our blessed grandfather."

The one who finds the coin is assured good fortune in the coming year. The coin is used to buy a candle for the church to be lighted on Christmas Day.

The table is not cleared after the meal in hopes that St. Basil will share the repast. And a Christmas cake with a cross on top is left on the table during Holy Night in hopes that Christ will come to eat it. After eating, the family gathers about the fireplace for an evening of storytelling, games, and fortunetelling.

To tell the future of two lovers, two olive leaves, named for the girl and boy concerned, are placed on hot embers in the fire. The way they curl indicates the course of love. If they curl toward each other, all is well. If they curl away, the couple will be unhappy together. If they burst into flame immediately, a long happy life together is promised.

The Christmas log must burn all night, and the fire must not go out until Epiphany in order to ward off the Karkantzari who are mischievous half-human, half-animal beings. They wander around from Christmas to Epiphany and stir up trouble especially for over-eaters who fall asleep. They cause wife trouble, bad children, make milk sour, and cause horses and donkeys to go lame. They are kept under control by sprinkling holy water throughout the house, a ritual the Orthodox Greek priest performs. Old shoes are burned in the fire for this purpose, too. The odor of burning leather is supposed to keep these creatures away.

## HOLLAND

Christmas is strictly a religious holiday marked by a family dinner and social visiting in Holland.

Once the children are in bed, St. Nicholas may drop by with surprise packages for the older people. He thumps the door knocker, then disappears, leaving the gifts. Packages are made as mysterious as possible. The giver often disguises his identity through riddles and rhymes. Sometimes a package is made up of many boxes with a different name on each layer so that it gets passed around many times before the true owner gets it.

During the "unwrapping" tea and hard cookies are traditionally served. Afterwards, the table is laden with "letter-banket," small cakes in the form of initials, hot chocolate, and buttered and salted roasted chestnuts. *"Klaasjes,"* flat, hard cookies originally baked in the form of St. Nicholas on his white horse but now made in various forms such as fish, birds, and animals, are traditionally served too.

Marzipan is a favorite Christmas candy in Holland. An old custom was for a young man to send his girl a marzipan Dutch boy as a gift. If she liked him, she would return a marzipan Dutch girl to him.

## HUNGARY

Some areas in Hungary celebrate St. Lucia's Day, December 13, to begin the Christmas season. Groups of boys chanting religious songs visit the farmhouses. It was thought that the fertility of geese and hens was assured by this custom. The boys were rewarded with cookies and cake for their efforts.

Christmas Eve ended the period of fasting, and an extra place was set at the evening meal for the stranger who might knock at the door seeking hospitality.

Family visiting and parties were popular and fortunetelling was practiced on these occasions.

At midnight a girl in search of a husband would sweep the crumbs from the Christmas Eve supper from the floor and throw them across the threshold. She was supposed to see her future husband's face before her as she threw the crumbs.

And on Christmas Eve a bowl of water was placed outside the house to freeze. The pattern formed in the ice was supposed to foretell the future spouse's occupation.

Another fortunetelling device was to cut an apple in two through the middle. If the pattern was a star-shaped one, it meant good health. But a broken pattern meant that sickness would follow.

Ashes from the Yule log were collected and placed at the foot of fruit trees to ensure a good harvest.

## IRELAND

The Irish custom of "feeding the wren" on December 26 is based on the legend of St. Stephen. Legend has it that St. Stephen attempted to hide in a bush from his enemies. He would have been

safe but was betrayed by a chattering wren who gave away his position. To help the wren do penance for this treason, Irish children
took a wren in a cage from door to door, collecting money for
charity.

It is also customary for the man of the house to set a two-foot
red Christmas candle decorated with holly sprigs in the main window of the house at Christmas time. The youngest child has the
honor of lighting the candle. Some homes display a candle for each
member of the family.

Cakes baked on Christmas Eve and eaten during the season were
thought to bring good luck and good health, so a cake was baked
on Christmas Eve for each member of the household. They usually
were circular and flavored with caraway seeds. If anyone's cake
broke, it was thought to be an omen of bad luck. This superstition
prevailed in England and Scotland too, and cakes such as these
were baked and eaten there for the same reason.

On New Year's Eve the man of the house customarily took a
loaf of bread and struck the door of the house, and the cowshed
too if there was one, and said three times, "Out with misfortune."

## ITALY

Because of the location of the papacy in Rome, pagan customs
were pretty much stamped out in Italy. St. Francis of Assisi created the famous tableau, forerunner of our modern day crib, in the
year 1223, in the little village church of Greccio. A dramatic representation of the stable at Bethlehem with live animals was shown to
the people, and soon the idea of the manger scene, to emphasize
the real meaning of Christmas, spread throughout the world.

The weeks before Christmas are spent in spiritual preparation for
the season of Advent. Shepherds come to the villages and towns to
salute the shrine of the Virgin with bagpipes. Afterwards they play
salutes at the homes of carpenters in honor of St. Joseph.

Eight days before Christmas, a special novena of prayers and
special church services begins. It ends on Christmas Day. Children
go from house to house reciting Christmas poems and are rewarded
with coins. Twenty-four hours before Christmas a strict fast is observed after which a meal of many dishes, but no meat, is served.

The traditional Christmas dinner, Cennone, is held on December 24. The table is laden with spaghetti and anchovies, an assortment of fish, fresh broccoli, tossed salad, fruits, and sweets.

Christmas Eve is a family time. A Yule log, the Appo, is burned, and toasts in wine and wishes for the future are expressed.

The Urn of Fate is an old Italian Christmas tradition. A large ornamental bowl becomes the receptacle of wrapped gifts for members of the family. When the family assembles, each member takes his turn drawing a gift from the urn until all the presents are distributed.

## LITHUANIA

Christmas Eve dinner, Kūčia, is the highlight of the day. The table is spread with fresh, sweet hay as a reminder of Christ's manger. Then it is covered with a snow-white cloth used only for this occasion. A plate of holy wafers, *plotkelēs,* and a crucifix are placed in the center of the table. As soon as the evening star appears in the sky, Kūčia begins.

The head of the family says a prayer of thanksgiving for past blessings of the year and adds the wish that things will be well in the year to come. Then he breaks and shares the wafers with each member of the family, and they, in turn, with each other. These wafers are known as "bread of the angels." Scenes of the Nativity are imprinted on them.

Twelve courses are served at the dinner symbolizing the Twelve Apostles. There are soup, fish, vegetables, small hard biscuits served with poppy seed and honey sauce, oatmeal pudding, and other dishes as well.

Straws are drawn from under the tablecloth. For older people the length of the straw indicates the length of life. Single people find the length of time before they will marry.

Girls carry bundles of kindling wood into the house. They count the amount of sticks they have brought. An even number of sticks in their bundle indicates marriage during the year.

Children run to the well to taste the water, or to the barn to listen to the animals. It was thought that for a time on Christmas Eve water would change into wine and animals would talk in the language of man.

The family attends Shepherd's Mass at midnight, but Christmas Day is spent at home or visiting neighbors. Before being admitted to a home, visitors are required to sing a Christmas carol. Only children receive gifts on Christmas.

## MEXICO

On December 16, Mexican homes are decorated with flowers, evergreens, and colored paper lanterns. A Nativity scene is set up in a prominent place in the house.

And so begins the *posada,* meaning resting place, commemorating Mary's and Joseph's journey and their unsuccessful efforts to find lodging for the night.

Groups assemble and go from door to door carrying candles and chanting a song asking for shelter. Of course they are told there is no room. This seeking continues each day until Christmas Eve.

In some homes the group divides in two, one half representing the Holy Pilgrims, the other the Hardhearted Innkeepers. The Pilgrims, led by a white-clad figure representing an angel, go through the house chanting. The Innkeepers, in a room designated as the inn, refuse them entry. After much persuading the Pilgrims win over the Innkeepers, and everyone kneels before an improvised altar with its Nativity scene and prays.

Then a party with singing, dancing, and games ensues. The traditional *piñata* is featured. This is a large earthenware jar filled with candy, nuts, fruits, and small gifts which has been decorated to look like a rooster, bull, clown's face, or whatever shape is desired.

The *piñata* is hung by a long rope from the ceiling, and the children are blindfolded, turned around a few times, then given three chances each to break the *piñata* with a stick. When the *piñata* does break, the goodies inside are shared by all.

The guests are served a meal of fruits, vegetables garnished with gaily colored candies, turkey, tortillas, fried peppers, chocolate, and coffee. Champagne is sometimes served too, and souvenirs are given to guests.

## NORWAY

Norwegian housewives are busy in the kitchen in the days before Christmas preparing the traditional foods: sausage, breads, cheese, cookies, and specialty dishes for the huge Christmas Day dinner.

Meats are also dried and salted at this time for the year's supply.

Flat *bröd,* a thin bread made of oat flour and baked slowly over a peat fire, is made in quantity at Christmas time so that there will be a supply on hand for the entire year. A Christmas breakfast specialty is *lefse,* made of mashed potato, salt, cream, and flour. It is rolled piecrust thin and baked like a waffle, then served with syrup and sausage. A favorite Christmas dessert is rice pudding and lingonberries served with many varieties of cookies.

Children are busy too, making candles for the Christmas tree.

Animals are given extra rations at Christmas, and a sheaf of wheat dipped in suet is hung outside for the birds.

The Peace of Christmas (Julafred) is publicly proclaimed. Children go to church early in the morning, while adults attend later. The family traditionally gathers around the fireplace for storytelling in the evening after a day of feasting.

People are on the watch during the Christmas season for Julenissen, those invisible troublemaking elves who ride on Jule-buken (goats) and cause mischief and bump bad children.

## PHILIPPINE ISLANDS

Lighted paper lanterns are strung outside the house for color, and children place their shoes in the window for the Three Kings to fill. On Christmas Eve carolers roam the streets, and families gather in their homes to celebrate the occasion.

## POLAND

The Christmas fast ends when the first star appears in the evening sky on December 24. Thus begins the Festival of the Star.

Straw is spread under the table where dinner will be eaten, in memory of the stable in Bethlehem, and a chair is left vacant for the Holy Child.

Before the meal the tradition of the Peace Wafer is observed. These are round, small flat wafers similar to Communion wafers. They have been blessed previously by the priest. The head of the family gives each person at the table a wafer and they exchange good wishes. This symbolizes the friendship and peace of all those in attendance and comes from the ancient tradition of "breaking bread." If any members of the household are absent, wafers are mailed to them.

Traditionally, dishes of mush, vegetables, fish, and almonds are included in the meal. No meat is served. Token gifts such as cookies, sugar hearts, and a silver coin are placed at each place setting.

After supper the Star Man (village priest) examines the children on their religious knowledge, and they receive small gifts from the Wise Men if they do well. The Wise Men are impersonated by three young men who carry a star and sing carols. In rural areas young people accompany the Wise Men, dressed as animals or characters from the Nativity scene symbolizing those privileged to attend the birth of the Christ Child. They go from house to house singing carols and receiving a glass of wine and cookies as welcome. Some groups carry small stages and give puppet shows on various Bible scenes.

Highways are decked throughout the Christmas season with Nativity scenes.

## QUEBEC, CANADA

This Canadian province follows ancient French Christmas customs.

Christmas Day begins with a midnight Mass, then Réveillon, the supper after attending church. The table is gaily set with ham, turkey, native dishes, nuts, fruits, sweets, wines, and liqueurs.

Gifts are exchanged on New Year's Day, and the season ends with the Feast of the Kings on Epiphany.

The traditional cake is Le Gâteau des Rois. A pea and a bean are baked into this cake. The two who get them are made King and Queen of Twelfth Night.

## ROMANIA

The festival in Romania begins when the first star on Christmas Eve is sighted. The parish priests make the rounds touring the districts to bless homes and the animals for the coming year.

Candles are lighted, and boys go caroling from house to house, their leader carrying a large wooden star (Steava) mounted on a long pole. The star is covered with gilt paper and colored streamers, and small bells are fastened onto it. There is a painting of the

Holy Family in the center of the star and a small candle placed inside to make the picture glow.

This night signifies an end to two weeks of fasting. Candles are lighted and a cube of incense is burned. The table is laden with food. The head of the household customarily holds a loaf of bread high over his head and prays that his wheat in the coming season will grow as high as that loaf. Each guest breaks off a piece of the bread, and the one who happens to get the biggest piece can expect to be lucky in the year to come.

## RUSSIA

Before the revolution there were many colorful customs practiced in Russia at Christmas time.

Fasting ended with the appearance of the evening star on Christmas Eve. It was a signal for supper (Colatzia) to begin. The table was covered with straw as a reminder of the Holy Child's manger. Christmas loaves often were eaten with syrup or honey before the main meal on Christmas Eve. And a thin wafer of white flour which had been blessed was divided among the family and friends at the table to symbolize the good will and peace of the season. The main meal always included dishes of fish and special cakes.

After dinner people formed processions wearing costumes representing the animals that had been present in the stable at Bethlehem. They roamed through the village singing carols, many of which were heathen sacrificial songs from the old days before Christianity.

At midnight there were church services, and the following day was for visiting neighbors and friends and having parties and dancing.

Fortunetelling was a popular pastime at these parties. The older women would interpret the future of someone if he dropped melted lead or wax into the snow. They made their predictions by analyzing the form the lead or wax took when it landed.

Another method of foretelling the future was to place five piles of grain on the kitchen floor. Each pile signified something about the future. Wealth, marriage, hope, charcoal for illness or death, and thread for a life of toil. A hen was brought into the room by the girl whose fortune was to be told. The pile the hen went to first upon release indicated the coming future of the girl.

Still another method of foretelling the future was used by experienced readers. An egg yolk was dropped into a glass of water to remain undisturbed overnight. The following day the discolorations were interpreted and were said to reveal the future of the person who had dropped the egg.

## SCOTLAND

A cake is baked on Christmas Eve for each member of the household. These are circular and are flavored with caraway seeds. If anyone's cake breaks, it is an omen of bad luck. Cakes baked on Christmas Eve and eaten during the season are thought to bring good luck and good health.

The first person to enter the house on Christmas morning customarily shouts, "First Footing," and presents a gift to the household to ensure future happiness for all in it. The First Footer is then given a stiff drink, which he must down in one gulp. The personality of the First Footer is important. A man with black hair is the most desired. A robust, cheerful man is a good sign too. And, of course, he should be a hearty drinker!

Anyone leaving the house on this day must remember to bring a gift with him if he plans to return during the day. It need not be an elaborate gift. Some food or a stick of wood for the fire would do. But he must bring something to be admitted.

The New Year's table is decorated with coal for a warm house, evergreen boughs for long life, and a loaf of bread for a full larder. A late supper is served of meat pies, scones, little Scottish pancakes eaten with butter and jam, ginger wine, and port. Of course there are singing and dancing of the Scottish reels.

## SPAIN

In some areas children expecting the Three Kings to leave them their Christmas gifts march to the gates of the city carrying cakes for the kings, figs for the servants, and hay for the mounts. They hope to see the kings silhouetted on distant hilltops as they journey to Bethlehem. But when it grows dark, the children return home to eat the food themselves. Later in the evening they go to church with their parents for services.

After midnight Mass on Christmas Eve, people crowd in the

streets singing and dancing to celebrate the holiday. At home children sing carols to the accompaniment of guitars and tambourines around the crib. This type of celebrating goes on until Twelfth Night.

The Urn of Fate is used in Spain too, but differently from in Italy. Gifts are not placed in it; names of friends, written on slips of paper, are put there instead. Two names are drawn at a time, and these people are expected to be especially friendly during the new year.

## SWEDEN

The Christmas season begins in Sweden with St. Lucy's Day, December 13. The eldest girl in the household dresses in white, with a red sash, and wears an evergreen crown with nine candles on it. Her duty on Christmas morning is to wake the family and bring them cakes and coffee.

St. Lucy was an early Christian martyr who refused to give up her religion to marry a pagan. She was burned at the stake by Emperor Diocletian. Her story was brought to Sweden by missionaries, and it appealed to the people, so she became the patron saint of all maidens. Her feast day fell on the same day as a pagan rite to the goddess of light, and so Lucy wears a crown of candles in remembrance of that ceremony.

Many communities choose a Lucia Queen and hold a pageant and parade in St. Lucy's honor.

Julafred, the Peace of Christmas, is publicly proclaimed in Sweden. Children go to church early in the morning, while adults attend later on. Christmas dinner begins with smorgasbord.

A full length centerpiece arrangement of oranges, raisins, tangerines, apples, nuts, pine boughs and cones, and candles in wooden toadstool candleholders to symbolize good luck in the new year is set on the table. Then the foods are piled on. There is a large assortment of cheeses, anchovies, herring, spiced fish, and caviar. A dried cod called *Lutfisk* is served with milk gravy. Roast pig with a caramel-colored sugar icing, goose, veal loaf, brown beans, liver pâté, and *Julglogg,* usually called *glogg,* coffee, and cookies end the feast.

The family then gathers around the fireplace for storytelling and enjoying each other's company.

In rural areas the animals are not forgotten. Farm animals are given extra rations at this time, and bundles of grain are tied to long poles and set up outdoors so that the birds can feast out of the reach of cats.

Legend has it that at midnight on Christmas Eve the animals may speak to add their homage to the Infant Jesus.

## SWITZERLAND

In French Switzerland the family attends midnight Mass and then returns home for supper. Tales are told of Christmas miracles when dumb animals are granted the power of human speech at midnight. Carols are yodeled and cowbells rung on Christmas Day, and children go from door to door to receive small gifts from their neighbors.

In rural areas many folk traditions are associated with Christmas.

On Christmas Eve, Grandmother picks the best onion she can find and cuts it in half. She peels off twelve layers, one for each month of the coming year. She fills each peeling with salt. The next morning she inspects the condition of the salt in each peeling and forecasts the weather to come for each month. Dry salt indicates good fair weather. Damp salt shows there will be rain.

Father goes to the orchard to tie bands of straw around the trunks of fruit trees to ensure a good crop during the coming year.

On Christmas Eve young girls take steps to ensure their future happiness. They visit nine different fountains and take three sips of water from each, while the church bells call the faithful to midnight Mass. Then, it is said, the girls will find their future husbands waiting for them at the church door.

On New Year's Day farmers consult the sky for omens. A red sky is an omen of storms, fires, and war.

And it is considered good luck to meet men or children on that day, but to avoid women!

## UKRAINE

Christmas begins with a forty-day fast ending on Christmas Eve. As soon as the evening star appears in the heavens, the family sits down at a straw-covered table, in memory of the manger scene, to partake of the Christmas wafer.

Christmas is really a Thanksgiving Day in the Ukraine to thank

God for a good harvest and to ask his blessing of the fields for the coming year.

The table the family sits at is straw-covered, and hay and straw are strewn on the floor. Two loaves of white bread are placed, one upon the other, on top of the hay on the table, and a Christmas candle is stuck into the upper loaf.

The father takes a sheaf of wheat from the barn to the house. He places it upright in a corner of the room. It is called Forefather, to symbolize those forefathers who first tilled the land.

A twelve-course dinner follows the eating of the Christmas wafer. Each course commemorates one of the Twelve Apostles. The first dish eaten is *"kutya,"* boiled wheat with honey and poppy seed. It is the most important dish served. The head of the family blesses it, then takes a spoonful and throws it against the ceiling. This is a pre-Christian symbol of Thanksgiving. Also included in the dinner are buckwheat and mushroom soup, pancakes in flax, cabbage, fish, prunes, special Christmas bread, and nuts. A honey porridge called *Koutia* is served to commemorate the Holy Crib. The porridge represents the straw in the manger. The honey, usually accompanied with fruit, symbolizes the Holy Child.

Everyone speaks in a low voice during the meal, using sweet tones to ensure a blessing for the house.

The Christmas season entails church services as well as visiting, singing, and dancing. Each day a singing group called the Kolyadniky goes caroling from house to house and receives refreshments for their efforts. The local priest visits his parishioners to bless each house and examine the children in their catechism.

Fortunetelling is very popular at this time of year. People look for spiders' webs in the house. To find one means good luck.

It is customary for a young girl to stand with her back to the gate of her home and kick a shoe into the air over her head. The direction the shoe points when it lands tells which direction her future husband will come from. But if the shoe points to the gate, she will not get married.

Another way of finding a future spouse is to arrange two lighted candles in front of two mirrors which face each other so that each candle is reflected in both mirrors. By looking hard and counting each reflection, one's future husband can be seen in back of the seventh image.

## YUGOSLAVIA

The Yule log is a very important symbol for Yugoslavians at Christmas time. It must be a large, strong young oak tree. It must be cut by the young men of the family at dawn of Christmas. It must fall toward the east when struck, at the exact moment of sunrise, and its branches must not touch those of surrounding trees. It must be large enough to burn for the entire Christmas season. If its fire should go out, a tragedy would surely befall the household.

All who help bring the Yule log home are safe from witchcraft during the year, so naturally every member of the household joins in the effort.

Once the log is burning, the family waits for Polaznik, a young man selected to play this role of first visitor to enter the house on Christmas morning.

When Polaznik arrives he first has to throw a handful of grain at each member of the family and ask a blessing on the household. Then the Yule log is struck. The number of sparks which fly up indicate the number of pigs, cattle, and sheep to be born in the coming year.

After this wine is poured on the Yule log as a token of thanksgiving for the harvest that was gathered. Then Polaznik leaves after placing a silver coin on the end of the log to assure food and good fortune for the family throughout the coming year.

Legend has it that angels proclaim the birth of the Infant King on Christmas Eve. They dip their wings into the water springs and purify the water for the coming year.

At dawn maidens fill their pitchers with the angel-blessed water, which is drunk on Christmas Day. A handful of corn and a sprig of basil are thrown into the spring to safeguard the purity of the blessed water and to ensure a good harvest.

# Chapter 6

# CHRISTMAS GAMES

In early days games were often tests of strength. They were competitions between contenders or a display of individual prowess. At times of celebrations they were entertainment as well as contests.

Blindman's Buff, forfeits, and hunt the slipper are very old games, sometimes called by different names but played by children all over the world. Originally they were to display a child's thinking ability and agility. Today, even though they are for fun, games still give participants a chance to compete against each other or against their own previous ability.

These are some games popular in other countries.

## BRAZIL

### Peteca

A *peteca* is a leather-covered trunk or bag. A small leather pouch full of sand, or a bean bag, can be used to play this game.

The first child tosses the bag into the air. He must keep hitting it into the air with one hand, not letting it fall to the ground. As he hits, he recites the alphabet. The player who gets through the most letters of the alphabet without missing the bag is the winner.

## CZECHOSLOVAKIA

### Candle Custom

Players place tiny candles in nutshells and light them. The shells are placed to float in a large bowl of water. The player whose candle burns the longest is the winner.

# DENMARK

## Bird's Alive

Players sit in a circle and pass a lighted stick from one to the other. If the stick stops burning, the player holding it must pay a forfeit. Players may blow on the stick to keep the fire alive. As they pass the stick they must say, "Bird's Alive!"

# ENGLAND

## Musical Parcels

A small gift is wrapped in masses of paper and string. Players are seated in a circle and the parcel is passed as music plays. When the music stops, the child holding the parcel tries to unwrap it. No tearing of paper or ripping of knots in the string is allowed. If the music starts again, the child must pass the parcel around the circle again, forfeiting his chance at reaching the gift. The game goes on until one child is able to unwrap completely the parcel and get the gift.

# GERMANY

## Chocolate Bar

A hat, scarf, gloves, knife, and fork are needed to play this game. Also a wrapped bar of chocolate and dice.

The players take turns throwing the dice. When one gets a double, he immediately puts on the hat, scarf, and gloves and tries to open the chocolate bar, using the knife and fork, and then to eat as much of it as he can, still using only the knife and fork. In the meantime the other players continue to throw the dice. If another player throws a double, then the player working on the chocolate bar must remove the hat, scarf, and gloves, and the new player puts them on to have his turn at trying his luck at the candy. The game goes on until someone has eaten all the candy.

# IRELAND

## Pass the Orange

Two teams are organized. The first player in each team places an orange beneath his chin and clasps his hands behind his back. When the signal is given, the first player in each team must pass the orange to the next member of his team standing behind him. No hands must be used, and the orange must be received under the chin of the next in line. The orange is passed back through the entire team. If the orange drops, the team must start over. The first team to pass the orange completely through its ranks successfully wins.

# SWEDEN

## Judge's Dance

Someone is picked to be It. The other players gather around It, giggling and teasing and trying to tempt him to laugh. He must keep a straight face or he is out of the game, and a new It is picked.

Here are some Christmas games played in the United States.

## Pin the Star on the Christmas Tree

Equipment:

Large picture of a Christmas tree
For each player, a paper star with player's name
   on the back, and with a pin through it

*Tack tree to the far wall. Start the line of children 6 feet away from the picture. Blindfold the first child in line and give him his star. He must then approach the picture and pin his star at the first spot that his hand touches. The winner is the child who pins his star to the top of the tree or closest to the top.*

## Santa's Club

*An older person is needed to play Santa because Santa knows the trick. The trick is to bring something that begins with the same letter as the child's first name. Santa explains that he has a club that everyone can join. But, to join, each child must offer a gift to Santa. Tell the children that there is a trick to the game and to listen carefully and they'll find it out. Then give an example. Say, "Richard can bring a radio. June can bring jam. Bob can bring balloons."*

*Then give each child a chance to join Santa's club.*

## Snowball Toss

Equipment:

3 Ping-Pong balls per player
Small box

*Place the box in the center of a circle of seated children. Going around the circle, each child tosses one ball as his turn comes. If the ball misses, it is returned to the thrower. The tossing is continued in rotation until one child has no more snowballs left. He is the winner.*

## Snowball Roll

Equipment:

Shoe box with 5 square openings cut along the edge of the long side of the box. Make the center opening the smallest and mark it 10 points over the top. Make 2 medium-sized end holes, marked 5 points. The other 2 holes make large and mark 1 point each.
3 marbles for each player

*Each player gets a chance to roll his 3 snowballs (marbles) at the box. The one who makes the highest score wins.*

## Icicle Hunt

Equipment:

Pieces of string of varying lengths

*Hide the icicles (strings). Have the children hunt for the icicles. The winner is the player whose strings form the longest line,* not *the player who collects the most string!*

## Star Race

Equipment:

Stars made of construction paper for each player
Half a straw for each player

*Set up start and finish lines. Line the players up on the start line; place a star on the floor in front of each one. The players must inhale on the straws to lift the stars and then walk across the room to deposit the star at the finish line. Player may touch the straw with his hands, but may not touch the star at all. If the star drops, the player must retrieve it by straw only and then continue with the game.*

## What Do You Hear?

Equipment:

Deck of cards for shuffling
Zipper for zipping
Elastic for snapping
Scissors for clipping
Cellophane for rattling
Phone dial for dialing
Door for slamming

Alarm clock for alarm ringing
Match for striking
Book for slamming shut
2 glasses, 1 filled with water, for pouring
1 hand for finger snapping
Paper and pencils for all players

*Seat players in front of the demonstrator so that they can't see the materials used. Demonstrate the sounds, and at each sound each player writes on a numbered sheet what he thought the sound was. The player who guesses the most sounds correctly wins.*

## Trim the Tree

Equipment:

Large drawing sheet for each team
Crayons for each team

*Divide the group into teams. At the signal the first player of each team goes to the team drawing sheet to start the game.*

*1st player must draw the tree*
*2nd  "     "    "  a stand for the tree*
*3rd  "     "    "    "  Christmas ball*

*Other players draw in turn: bell, star, tinsel, another ball, star,*

Plate I.  Why not a personalized Christmas tree?
*Celebrity Christmas Trees by Hallmark Gallery*
*design staff, New York.*

*bell, hanging cookie, Santa for the top of the tree, etc. The first team to complete the drawing wins.*

## Christmas Card Puzzle

Equipment:

For each player a Christmas card cut into irregular pieces

*The first player to piece together his card correctly wins.*

## Jingle Bells

Equipment:

Bell
Adult leader

*The players sit in a circle and pass the bell singing "Jingle Bells." When the leader calls, "Stop," the player caught with the bell is out. The last player to remain in the game wins.*

## Hanging the Stocking

Equipment:

Cord tied between 2 chairs placed 6 feet apart
12 clothespins for each player (representing stockings)

*Blindfold a player and hand stockings (clothespins) to him one at a time. The player must hang the stockings on the line using only one hand. The player getting the most stockings hung on the line wins.*

## Christmas Card Mixer

Equipment:

Old Christmas cards cut diagonally in half

*Give the girls the upper halves, the boys the lower halves. At the signal the players must find their partners. The first couple to do so wins.*

## Bringing in the Christmas Tree

Equipment:

Small paper Christmas tree pictures enough for about 5 for each
player

*Label each tree with points (5, 10, 15, 20, 25). Hide the trees. On a signal the players hunt for the trees. The player getting the most points, not the most trees, wins.*

## Christmas Gift Hunt

Equipment:

Small gift for each player with his name on it

*Each player must hunt for his own gift and take only the one addressed to him, not calling attention to the names or hiding places of others he may find.*

## Santa's Sack of Stunts

Equipment:

Sack with slips of paper suggesting things player is to do

*Each player draws a slip in turn and does what is written on the slip. (Pretend to be someone of the opposite sex getting dressed; pantomime a baseball player being struck out; pretend to be putting on a tie; pretend to feed a baby cereal; pretend you are a hungry dog; pretend to set your hair; pretend to cook a dinner.)*

## Christmas Present Relay

Equipment:

2 wrapped packages

*Set up 2 teams. The first runner of each team runs from the start line across the room, where he unties the wrapped gift. He then runs back to his team and touches the next player in line. This player then runs to the unwrapped gift and has to rewrap it. Then he runs back to the next teammate and touches him so that this player may begin the process again. The first team to complete the task wins.*

## Telegram to Santa

Equipment:

Pencils and paper

*Players choose partners. Each couple is given 3 minutes to write Santa a telegram using in order the letters SANTA CLAUS. The telegrams are then read to the group, and the best one wins.*

### Ice Cream Game

Equipment:

Plates of ice cream and spoons

*Players choose partners. They are given 2 plates of ice cream and 2 spoons, but the spoons are tied together by a 6-inch piece of string. They have to eat their ice cream under these conditions. The first couple to finish wins.*

### Gift-Carrying Relay

Equipment:

2 packages

*2 teams are formed. The first player of each team places a package on his head and must walk across the room, tag the opposite wall, then return to pass the gift to the next team member, who repeats the procedure. No hands may be used, except to hand the package to the next player. If the gift package falls, the contestant must stop and replace it. The first team to complete the task wins.*

### Bubble Package Game

Equipment:

Gift for each player
Bubble pipe for each player

*Small gift packages are placed on a table. The children circle the table and blow bubbles. If a bubble lands on a package, that gift belongs to the child who blew the bubble.*

This is a very old game which has been played by adults for many years at Christmas time.

### Snapdragon

*A quantity of raisins is placed in a large shallow bowl, and brandy is poured over them. Then the liquid is ignited. Players try to grasp raisins by plunging their hands through the flames. All lights in the room are turned out when the game is in progress to add to the atmosphere. The player who gets the most raisins wins.*

# Chapter 7

# RECIPES FOR INTERNATIONAL CHRISTMAS BREADS AND CAKES

In pre-Christian times the winter solstice was celebrated for ten to twelve days in December. One of the rituals was expressing reverence for the gift of bread so that the favor of the field gods was won for the new year of planting and reaping. Agricultural fertility cults in the ancient nations of Europe were universal. Invocations, displays of wheat in the home, and baking of special breads and cakes were part of the ritual. Many of these customs were carried over and became Christian practices. Even today the baking of certain breads and cakes is ritual for Christmas. It is a lovely custom, which when we think about it at other times of the year brings back the festivity of Christmas to our memory. Remember the Christmas *Stollen* your grandmother baked? Or was it a Yule log, spicecake, or fruitcake? Each country has its own specialty.

## ARMENIA

### Sugar Cakes

*Very good served with a hot cup of coffee.*

2 packages active dry yeast
½ cup lukewarm water
2 large potatoes, cooked,
    mashed
¾ cup milk
½ cup soft butter or margarine

4 cups sifted flour
½ teaspoon salt
2 eggs
½ cup sugar
¼ cup brown sugar

*Dissolve yeast in water. Add potatoes, milk, and ¼ cup butter or margarine. Blend until there are no lumps. Stir in flour and salt.*

*Beat eggs and sugar together, and add to the dough mixture. Mix well.*

*Cover with cloth wrung out in warm water, and place in 110°– 120° oven for 30 minutes.*

*Place dough in a greased 6-cup ring mold orange cake pan. Punch 12 (½ inch deep) holes into the dough with your fingers. Fill the holes with the remaining butter (¼ cup), and sprinkle with brown sugar. Bake at 350° oven for 35 minutes.* Yield: about 12 servings.

# AUSTRIA

## Christmas Stollen

### *My father's favorite!*

1 (13¾ ounce) package of hot roll mix
1 tablespoon sugar
½ cup water
1 egg, beaten
1 cup raisins
1 cup candied fruit
1 tablespoon dark rum

1 (14½ ounce) package gingerbread mix
1 egg, beaten
¼ cup milk
¾ cup blanched, sliced almonds
2 tablespoons sugar
¼ cup water

*Dissolve yeast from hot roll mix and sugar in water. Add beaten egg. Beat vigorously. Add dry ingredients of hot roll mix. Blend. Cover with cloth wrung out in warm water and place in 110°–120° oven for 30 minutes.*

*Meanwhile sprinkle raisins and fruit with rum. Let stand.*

*Prepare gingerbread mix, but use ½ cup ONLY.*

*Punch down hot roll dough. Turn out onto a floured board. Knead for 2–3 minutes. Roll out in a rectangle about 15" by 12". Spread gingerbread batter carefully onto rolled-out dough. Sprinkle with raisins and fruit. Roll dough from the long side, make a loose roll. Using two large spatulas, lift roll onto greased cookie sheet. Brush surface with a wash made up of 1 beaten egg and ¼ cup of milk.*

*Make slits 2" long and ½" deep lengthwise down the roll. Sprinkle with almonds. Bake in a 375° oven for 40–45 minutes. Remove from oven. Brush with 2 tablespoons sugar dissolved in ¼ cup water. Remove from pan. Cool on rack.*

## CANADA

### Rum Cake

*Delicious!*

¾ cup butter
1½ cups firmly packed light
   brown sugar
1 pound pitted, chopped dates
1 pound walnuts, shelled,
   chopped
1 teaspoon baking soda

1 cup boiling water
3 eggs, well beaten
2¼ cup sifted flour
1 teaspoon salt
2 tablespoons rum
Rum glaze (given below)

*Preheat oven to 300°.*
*Grease 13" by 9" by 2" pan.*
*Cream butter and sugar. Add dates and nuts. Mix soda and water. Pour over first mixture. Add eggs. Stir in flour and salt. Beat until smooth. Add rum and blend. Turn into pan. Bake at 300° oven for 1½ hours.*
*Cool slightly in pan for 10 minutes on a wire rack. Remove from pan. Frost with rum glaze.* Yield: 12 servings.

### Rum Glaze

¾ cup confectioners' sugar
2 teaspoons sugar
1 teaspoon rum

*Mix ingredients. Frost cake while still warm.*

## ENGLAND

### Trifle

*One of my favorites for a good-looking and delicious dessert.*

1 spongecake, thinly sliced
1 cup milk
Some sugar

Some vanilla
Stewed fruit or berries (not too
   sweet or too moist)

*Line a glass serving bowl with spongecake. Flavor a cup of milk with some sugar and vanilla to taste. Sprinkle this over the cake to moisten lightly. Spread fruits on cake and chill. When ready to serve pour custard sauce all over the cake.*

## Custard Sauce

4 egg yolks
1 cup sugar
2 cups milk

*Beat yolks in top of a double boiler. Beat in sugar and milk. Cook and stir over hot water. Chill. Makes a thickened golden sauce.*

Optional: *Decorate cake with whipped cream, nuts, fruits.*

## English Saffron Bread

*Lovely to look at, interesting to taste.*

1 (13¾ ounce) package hot roll mix
1 teaspoon powdered saffron
½ cup currants

½ cup chopped walnuts
1 egg, beaten
2 tablespoons sugar

*Prepare mix as directed on package. Add saffron. Cover with cloth wrung out in warm water and place in 110°–120° oven for 30 minutes.*
*Mix in currants and nuts.*
*Place dough in a 5" by 9" greased loaf pan. Brush with egg. Sprinkle sugar on. Bake in a 375° oven for 30–35 minutes.*

# FINLAND

## Joululuumukakku

*Pronounced "You-lulu-moo-ka-coo," this is the traditional Finnish Christmas cake.*

1 package active dry yeast
1⅓ cups lukewarm water
2 egg whites
1 (1 pound 2½ ounce) package white cake mix
½ pound pitted prunes

½ pound pitted apricots
½ cup sugar
1 teaspoon vanilla
½ cup cold water
1 (2 ounce) package topping mix, whipped

*Warm mixing bowl.*
*Use all ingredients at room temperature.*
*Dissolve yeast in water. Add egg whites to cake mix. Follow package directions for mixing cake. Cover with hot-water-dampened clean towel. Let rise in 110°–120° oven for 30 minutes.*

*Bake in 2 greased 8-inch layer cake pans for 45 minutes. Cool layers for 5 minutes in the pans. Finish cooling on wire racks.*

*Cook prunes, apricots, sugar, vanilla in ½ cup cold water for 10 minutes. Chop fruit except for 4 prunes and 4 apricots. Cool, then spread fruit between the layers of cake.*

*Frost the top and sides of the cake with topping. Decorate with remaining fruit.* Yield: 8–10 portions.

# FRANCE

## Yule Log

*One of the most decorative cakes to serve. Really dresses up the table and makes your guests oh and ah.*

2 bought jelly rolls
½ cup soft butter or margarine
¼ cup confectioners' sugar
1 egg yolk

1 (1 ounce) package chocolate, premelted
10 spearmint gumdrop leaves
12 red cinnamon candies

*Place jelly rolls end to end on a platter. Cut ends diagonally.*

*Cream butter and sugar until light and fluffy. Blend in egg yolk and chocolate. Beat until smooth.*

*Frost jelly roll to give it a bark-like appearance. Run a fork through the frosting, making wavy lines to create this effect.*

*Decorate with gumdrop leaves and candies across the top, making a holly pattern. Refrigerate until ready to serve. Yield: 8 portions.*

# GERMANY

## Coffee Braid

*Very festive-looking, and tasty, too.*

| | |
|---|---|
| 1 package active dry yeast | 3 cups sifted flour |
| 2 tablespoons very warm water (105°–115°) | 1½ teaspoons ground cinnamon |
| ¾ cup scalded milk | ¼ teaspoon ground nutmeg |
| ½ cup margarine | Confectioners' sugar frosting |
| ¾ cup sugar | (given below) |
| 1 teaspoon salt | Candied cherries |
| 1 egg | Chopped walnuts |

*Preheat oven to 350°.*

*Grease cookie sheet.*

*Sprinkle yeast into warm water. Let it stand for a few minutes. Then stir until it is dissolved.*

*Pour hot milk over ¼ cup margarine, ¼ cup sugar, and the salt. Cool until lukewarm. Add the yeast, egg, and 1½ cups flour. Beat until smooth. Then beat in the remaining flour.*

*Turn onto floured pastry board. Knead till smooth and satiny. Place in a greased bowl. Turn once and cover. Allow to rise for 1 hour, until doubled.*

*Punch down and allow to rise again. Divide in 3 equal parts and roll each part into a 12″ by 17″ rectangle. Brush with soft butter.*

*Mix ½ cup sugar, cinnamon, nutmeg. Sprinkle on the dough. Roll each piece tightly from the narrow side. Place on greased cookie sheet. Braid tightly. Pinch ends together. Brush with soft butter. Sprinkle with sugar. Let rise for about 30 minutes, until doubled.*

*Bake in 350° oven for 30 minutes. Cool. Decorate with confectioners' sugar frosting, cherries, and nuts.*

## Confectioners' Sugar Frosting

½ cup sifted confectioners' sugar
Some milk
A few drops vanilla flavoring

*Combine sugar with enough milk to make a thick pouring consistency. Stir in vanilla flavoring.*

# HOLLAND

## Kerstkrans

*This is the traditional Dutch Christmas pastry, a rich and luscious favorite.*

### Pastry

1⅓ cups unsifted flour
½ cup butter

3 tablespoons ice water
2 tablespoons soft butter

*Place flour in bowl. Cut in butter with a pastry blender until mixture looks like cornmeal. Sprinkle top with ice water. Blend with fork. Shape into a ball.*

*Roll dough out on a floured board to ⅛" thickness. Spread with 2 tablespoons butter evenly. Roll up pastry like a jelly roll. Flatten with a rolling pin to ¾" thickness. Fold in ends, making 3 layers. Chill for 1 hour.*

### Filling

1 cup finely ground, blanched
   almonds
½ cup sugar

1 egg
1 tablespoon lemon juice

*Mix almonds, sugar, egg, and lemon juice. Shape into 1" thick rolls. Coat with flour.*

*Now roll out pastry dough into a 5" by 20" rectangle. Place the small rolls of almond mixture in a line down the center. Bring sides of the dough over the filling to overlap. Paint the edges with water. Press the edges together and seal.*

*Shape the roll into a wreath. Fit the ends together. Place, seam down, on ungreased cookie sheet. Bake in a 400° oven for 40 minutes, until golden brown. Cool.*

**Glaze**

1 tablespoon cream
½ cup sifted powdered sugar

1 teaspoon lemon juice
Candied fruits and nuts

*Mix cream and sugar. Blend in lemon juice. Spoon glaze over the top of the pastry. Decorate with fruits and nuts.* Yield: 12 servings.

# HONDURAS

## Torrejas

*This is the traditional Christmas dessert, ladyfingers in syrup.*

1 cup light brown sugar, firmly
packed
1 cup water

2 cinnamon sticks
12 ladyfingers

*Boil sugar, water, and cinnamon sticks together for 10 minutes. Lay ladyfingers in a shallow dish. Pour the syrup over the ladyfingers. Let stand for 5 minutes, then serve hot.* Yield: 4–6 portions.

# HUNGARY

## Poppy Cakes

*If you like poppy seeds, this recipe will be a favorite.*

1 package active dry yeast
½ cup lukewarm water
1 egg, beaten
⅔ cup unsifted flour
½ cup raisins
½ cup sugar
⅓ cup poppy seeds

¼ cup milk
2 teaspoons grated lemon rind
⅓ cup chopped walnuts
1 (14 ounce) package coffeecake
mix
¼ cup confectioners' sugar

*Dissolve yeast in lukewarm water. Add egg and flour. Mix well. Cover with a cloth wrung out in warm water. Place in 110°–120° oven for 30 minutes.*

*Meanwhile, combine raisins, sugar, poppy seeds, milk, and rind in a saucepan. Cook over low heat until mixture is thick enough to spread.*

*Prepare coffeecake dough according to directions on package.*

*Fold walnuts, poppy seed mixture, and coffeecake dough into yeast mixture. Stir well. Place in a greased 6-cup ring mold. Bake at 350° for 45 minutes. Remove from oven.*

*Cool. Remove from pan. Sift confectioners' sugar over the top. Cut after the cake sits for several hours. Makes a ring loaf to serve about 12 people.* Yield: 12 portions.

# IRELAND

## Fruitcake

*If you need a cake that will stay fresh for days, this is it.*

1 cup soft shortening
2 cups brown sugar
4 large eggs
3 cups sifted flour
1 teaspoon baking powder

1 teaspoon salt
1 cup molasses
Candied fruits
Chopped nuts

*Line 2 (9" by 15" by 3") loaf pans with heavy wrapping paper and grease.*

*Cream shortening and sugar till fluffy. Beat in eggs. Sift flour, baking powder, and salt together. Stir gradually into egg mixture, alternating with portions of the cup of liquid molasses. Blend in fruits and nuts.*

*Fill both pans almost full. Bake in a 300° oven for 2½–3 hours, until toothpick stuck into cake comes out clean. Cover with greased paper for the last hour. Cool. Store wrapped in foil.* Yield: about 30 portions.

# ITALY

## Pannetone

*This is the traditional bread baked at Christmas by Italians.*

2 packages active dry yeast
½ cup lukewarm water
1½ cups lukewarm milk
3 eggs, beaten
⅓ cup sugar
¼ cup softened butter
1½ teaspoons salt
¼ teaspoon allspice

2 drops yellow food coloring
6 cups sifted flour
½ cup raisins
½ cup chopped, mixed candied fruit
⅓ cup chopped almonds
⅓ cup chopped, candied lemon rind

*Soften yeast in water. Add milk, eggs, sugar, butter, salt, allspice, and food coloring. Mix well.*

*Gradually mix in sifted flour. Cover with cloth wrung out in warm water and place in 110°–120° oven for 30 minutes.*

*Stir dough down. Add raisins, fruit, nuts, and rind. Stir and mix well.*

*Spoon dough into 3 well-greased 1-pound coffee cans. Bake in a 375° oven for 45 minutes. Let stand for 5 minutes before removing from cans.* Yield: 3 cakes (15 servings).

## Zuppa Inglese

*Which translates from the Italian as English soup and is similar to the English trifle. It is used as a famous Italian Christmas treat.*

1 (2¾ ounce) package egg custard mix
1½ cups eggnog
1 (12 ounce) package ladyfingers

¼ cup sherry
½ cup raspberry jam
½ cup chopped almonds
1 teaspoon cinnamon

*9″ square greased cake pan.*

*Prepare egg custard mix using eggnog instead of stated amount of milk. No extra egg yolk is needed. Cool and allow to thicken.*

*Split package of ladyfingers and line cake pan with them. Sprinkle with sherry until cake is wet, not soggy. Spread jam over bottom.*

*Pour cooled custard over jam. Top with almonds and sprinkle with cinnamon. Chill in refrigerator for 4 hours before serving.* Yield: 6 portions.

# MALAYA

### Spiku

*This is a tasty Malayan 6-layer cake.*

| | |
|---|---|
| 12 tablespoons butter | ¾ cup sifted flour |
| 6 tablespoons sugar | 1½ teaspoons nutmeg |
| 12 eggs, separated | 1½ teaspoons cinnamon |

*Preheat oven to 400°.*

*Grease 3 8″ layer cake pans, and line bottoms with waxed paper.*

*Cream 6 tablespoons butter with the sugar. Add beaten egg yolks. Beat well. Beat in flour and spices. Fold in stiffly beaten egg whites. Divide batter in half.*

*Divide half of the batter among the 3 pans. Bake in a 400° oven for 8–10 minutes.*

*Remove cakes from pans. Spread each with 1 tablespoon butter. Bake another 3 pans of cake with the remaining batter. Spread with remaining butter again as before. Put layers together to make a 6-layer cake.*

# MEXICO

### Holiday Cake

*This cake is served after Posadas and the* piñata *party.*

| | |
|---|---|
| 1 (1 pound, 10 ounce) package poundcake mix | ½ teaspoon cinnamon |
| 1½ cups light corn syrup | ¼ teaspoon ground cloves |
| 1 (4 ounce) can shredded coconut | 2 eggs, beaten |
| | ¼ cup milk |
| 2 tablespoons sherry | 2 tablespoons butter |

*Prepare cake as directed on package.*

*To prepare coconut syrup, boil corn syrup for 2 minutes, then add coconut, sherry, cinnamon, and cloves. Mix well. Turn heat off but keep warm.*

*When the cake is cool, cut it into 12 ¼" thick slices. Beat the eggs with the milk. Dip the cake slices into this mixture. Sauté both sides of the slices in butter until golden brown.*

*Pour warm coconut syrup over the slices before serving.* Yield: 12 portions.

# NORWAY

## Christmas Buns

1 (13¾ ounce) package hot roll mix
½ cup raisins
1 teaspoon grated lemon rind
1 teaspoon ground cardamom
¼ teaspoon allspice
1 egg, beaten
1 teaspoon water
Icing

*Warm mixing bowl.*
*Use ingredients at room temperature.*
*Prepare mix as package directs. Cover with a cloth wrung out in warm water. Let dough rise in a 110°–120° oven for 30 minutes. Add raisins, rind, cardamom, and allspice. Blend well.*
*Divide dough into 12 pieces. Shape to fit into 12 greased 3¼" fluted tart tins. Glaze with egg, beaten with water. Bake in a 375° oven for 30 minutes.*

## Icing

½ cup confectioners' sugar
1 tablespoon water
½ teaspoon lemon juice

*Make icing from sugar, water, and lemon juice. Spoon onto buns while they are warm.*

## Kransekake

*This is used in Norway at Christmas time because of its gay tree shape.*

### Cookie ring pattern:

*Use a compass to make the rings. Number the pattern to keep rings in order. For the first layer make a circle 1" in diameter. For the second layer a circle 1¼" in diameter. For the third layer a circle 1½" in diameter, and so on until you have 25 paper circles. Each one should be ¼" larger than the one before.*

### Recipe for cake:

2 cups soft butter
1 cup almond paste
2 cups sifted powdered sugar
2 teaspoons almond extract

4 egg yolks, well beaten
5 cups sifted flour
Bought marzipan fruits
Toothpicks

*Preheat oven to 350°.*
*Use pastry bag or cookie press with plain tip ½" in diameter.*
*Lightly grease cookie sheets.*
*Cream butter, almond paste, sugar, and almond extract until smooth. Add egg yolks. Add flour gradually. Mix till very smooth.*
*Place patterns on cookie sheet. Put dough into pastry bag or cookie press. Press out, forming rings around inside edges of the pattern, beginning with the smallest. Chill for 15 minutes.*
*Bake in a 350° oven for 15 minutes or till delicately browned. Cool on sheet.*
*To create the cake, place largest ring on a plate, top with next largest ring, and so on. Stack rings until all 25 layers are used. To decorate this tall tree-shaped cake, stick toothpicks into the marzipan fruits and place the other end of the pick between the layers to hold the fruits in place. To serve, lift off each layer. For larger layers, cut into serving-sized pieces. Yield: 30–35 portions.*

## PUERTO RICO

### Tipsy Cake

*This is called* sopa borracha *in Puerto Rico. It makes a pretty cake as well as a tasty one.*

3 cups sugar
2 cups water
1½ cups muscatel
½ pound spongecake

2 egg whites, stiffly beaten
1 tablespoon tiny multicolored
    candies

*Combine 2½ cups sugar and the water. Boil until a heavy syrup forms (240° on a candy thermometer). Remove from the heat. Add the wine. Stir.*

*Cut the cake into 2" squares. Place in individual custard cups. Pour syrup over the squares. Add the remaining sugar to the beaten egg whites. Beat until fluffy. Use this meringue as cake topping. Sprinkle candies on the top of the meringue. Serve cold.* Yield: 8 portions.

## RUSSIA

### Walnut Cake

*This cake is called* mazourka *in Russian and is excellent with coffee or as a tasty snack.*

9 egg yolks
2 cups sugar
9 egg whites
3 cups flour
1 pound ground walnuts

½ pound ground candied fruit
    rind
2 tablespoons lemon juice
Some powdered sugar

*Preheat oven to 325°.*

*Butter and lightly flour 8" by 12" flat pan.*

*Beat egg yolks in bowl. Add sugar. Beat well. In separate bowl beat egg whites till stiff (not dry). Fold into yolk mixture. Add flour, nuts, fruit rind, and lemon juice. Mix lightly.*

*Bake in a 325° oven for 30 minutes. Dust with powdered sugar when cool. Cake will be 1" high. Cut into long, thin slices.* Yield: 24 portions.

## SWEDEN

### Lussekake

*It's an old Swedish custom to awaken at dawn for coffee and lussekake on St. Lucy's Day.*

1 (13¾ ounce) package hot roll mix
½ teaspoon saffron
Raisins

*Make roll mix and flavor with saffron. Roll dough to 18" by 12" on floured surface. Then cut 1" by 9" strips. Form in S shapes. Coil ends in snail fashion. Place a raisin in the center of each. Bake according to roll mix instructions.* Yield: 24 portions.

### Limpa

1 (12 ounce) bottle beer
2 packages active dry yeast
1 cup warm milk
3 cups sifted flour
5 cups sifted rye flour

2 cups molasses
1 teaspoon sugar
4 tablespoons grated orange rind
1 cup chopped walnuts

*Use warm mixing bowl.*
*Use all ingredients at room temperature.*
*Boil beer for 5 minutes. Let cool till lukewarm.*
*Dissolve 1 package of yeast in milk. Stir in 3 cups flour and 2 cups rye flour, molasses, and sugar. Cover with cloth wrung out in warm water and place in a 110°–120° oven for 30 minutes.*
*Dissolve second package of yeast in warm beer. Stir in 3 cups rye flour and orange rind. Cover bowl with damp cloth. Place in a 110°–120° oven for 30 minutes.*
*Now mix the 2 doughs together, adding the walnuts. Divide dough into 3 (2½ cup) portions. Put in 3 greased 4½" by 8½" loaf pans. Bake at 375° for 45 minutes. Remove from pans. Cool thoroughly before slicing.* Yield: 3 loaves.

## UNITED STATES

### Heavenly Cranberry Pie

1 (3 ounce) package lemon
flavor gelatin
1 cup boiling water
2 cups fresh cranberries
½ cup water

½–¾ cup sugar
1 envelope topping mix,
whipped
1 baked 8″ crumb crust or cooled
pastry shell

*Dissolve gelatin in boiling water. Combine cranberries and ½ cup water in a saucepan. Cook and stir over medium heat until cranberry skins burst. Add sugar and cook for 3–5 minutes longer over low heat. Drain cranberries, reserving juice. Stir cranberry juice into gelatin mixture and chill until thickened. Prepare topping mix as directed on package. Stir cranberries into thickened gelatin mixture, then fold in prepared whipped topping. Chill again until mixture mounds. Pour into crumb crust or pastry shell. Chill until ready to serve.* Yield: about 6 portions.

# Chapter 8

# RECIPES FOR INTERNATIONAL CHRISTMAS COOKIES

Many countries have added or substituted the making of Christmas cookies, pastries, and candies for the ancient tradition of making Christmas breads or cakes. Each country has its own specialties, and in the United States you will find recipes being used from all over the world. They were brought here with the waves of immigrants, became popular, and have crossed national lines ever since. Today we hardly remember their origins. We only know that they taste good!

When it comes to cookie making, the only *real* problem the world over is keeping the cookie jar filled! In my house, as soon as the fragrance of cookie baking fills the kitchen, the family comes running to sample. At Christmas it is wise to make a little extra for them to taste if you want to have any left to put away for gift giving or serving.

The wonderful thing about preparing cookies is that you can make them in advance on a day when you are not rushed by other duties. You can store them if Christmas is within a week, or freeze them until holiday time.

## TIPS:

When you store cookies, remember to store the crisp ones separately from the soft ones. Crisp cookies are kept best in a can with a loose cover. If they should get soft, you can crisp them again by placing them in a moderate oven for a few minutes.

Soft cookies should be kept in an airtight container. To keep them moist, you can place a slice of apple or bread in the container with them.

To keep for longer periods of time, cookies can be frozen either baked or unbaked. If they are baked, they should store up to 12 months. Frozen dough will store up to 6 months.

When freezing baked cookies seal them in a freezer container when they have cooled. When ready to use leave them in the covered container until completely thawed.

In freezing dough seal in freezer containers till ready to use.

At baking time, for best results, use flat baking sheets with low, or no, sides. Light-colored, shiny pans produce the best cookie results.

Remember, ovens vary because of differences in insulation. A cookie may take less time to bake in a well-designed oven, or more time in a poorly insulated one. You know your oven, so judge time accordingly.

Colorful packaging always makes a gift more exciting. Cookies, since they are attractive in themselves, can be arranged on a large paper plate with a Christmas design and sealed by see-through plastic wrap.

A cookie candle makes a pretty gift. You can stack flat cookies of the same size and wrap them in cylinder form in red or green foil or plastic wrap. Then you can insert a piece of gold foil cut in flame shape at the top of the package.

Plastic berry boxes laced with colorful Christmas ribbon make attractive cookie containers too, as do apothecary jars.

Of course, any paper or tin can can be covered with Christmas paper to make a wonderful cookie box.

If you wish to serve your cookies, you can use a colored Styrofoam tree form. Insert toothpicks or popsicle sticks in small or ball-type cookies, and decorate the tree by pinning the cookies to it.

Plate II shows an assortment of cookies that are favorites at Christmas.

Cookies always look good, but sometimes it is interesting to arrange an international assortment for gift giving or serving. The following recipes will provide enough variety for such a selection, or for just a colorful, tempting arrangement.

# AUSTRIA

## Crescents

*Austrian women are noted bakers. Try these and you'll know why.*

| | |
|---|---|
| 1 cup butter | 2 cups flour |
| ½ pint small-curd, dry cottage cheese | ¼ teaspoon salt |
| | 1 cup berry jam |
| 1 tablespoon sour cream | Milk |

*Heat oven to 400°.*

*Cream butter. Blend in cheese (which has been forced through a fine sieve) and sour cream. Add sifted flour and salt. Chill for 2 hours.*

*Roll dough thin, a portion at a time, on a lightly floured board. Cut in 3″ squares, then in triangles. Place jam in center of each piece, then roll and curve the rolled dough into crescent shapes. Place on ungreased baking sheet. Brush top with milk. Bake in 400° oven for 20 minutes.* Yield: 2½ dozen.

# BRAZIL

## Coffee Cookies

*If coffee flavoring is your favorite, you'll love these.*

| | |
|---|---|
| ⅓ cup shortening | 2 cups flour |
| ½ cup packed brown sugar | ½ teaspoon salt |
| ½ cup granulated sugar | ½ teaspoon soda |
| 1 egg | ¼ teaspoon baking powder |
| 1½ teaspoons vanilla | 2 tablespoons powdered instant coffee |
| 1 tablespoon milk | |

*Heat oven to 400°.*

*Mix shortening, sugars, egg, vanilla, and milk until fluffy. Sift in flour. Stir remaining dry ingredients together. Add to sugar mixture. Mix well.*

*Shape dough in 1″ balls. (If too soft, chill.) Place balls 2″ apart on ungreased baking sheet. With a greased fork dipped in sugar*

*flatten to ⅛″ thickness. Press in one direction only. Bake in a 400°
oven for 8–10 minutes, until lightly browned. Yield: 4 dozen.*

# CANADA

## Almond Cookies

*Our neighbors to the north have combined the art of English and
French baking to give us this delicious addition to the cookie jar.*

6 tablespoons butter
1 cup brown sugar
¼ cup cold water
1¾ cups sifted flour

1 teaspoon soda
½ teaspoon salt
½ teaspoon cinnamon
½ cup cut, blanched almonds

*Heat oven to 400°.*

*Mix butter and sugar. Stir in water. Sift together flour, soda, salt,
cinnamon, and stir in. Add almonds and mix thoroughly with hands.*

*Press and mold into smooth roll 2½″ in diameter. Wrap in waxed
paper. Chill until stiff (several hours).*

*Cut into ⅛″ thick slices. Place slices slightly apart on ungreased
baking sheet. Bake in a 400° oven for 6–8 minutes, until lightly
browned. Remove from sheet immediately. Yield: 4 dozen.*

# CHINA

## Chestnut Balls

*Chinese recipes are handed down from generation to generation.
Here are two good ones that you can start handing down.*

2 pounds chestnuts
½ cup honey

¾ cup confectioners' sugar
1 teaspoon cinnamon

*Cut crosses into the top of each chestnut shell. Boil in water until
shells burst. Drain. Cool. Shell. Force through food mill. Blend in
honey. Form into walnut-sized balls. Roll in mixture of confectioners'
sugar and cinnamon. Yield: 18 balls.*

## Chinese Chews

¾ cup flour
¼ teaspoon salt
1 teaspoon baking powder
1 cup sugar

1 cup chopped dates
1 cup chopped walnuts
3 eggs, well beaten

*Heat oven to 300°.*
*Grease 10" by 14" pan.*
*Sift dry ingredients. Stir in remaining ingredients. Pour into greased pan. Bake in a 300° oven for 30 minutes.* Yield: approx. 30 squares.

# ENGLAND

## Rolled Wafers

*Just about everyone is familiar with the English custom of "tea." With it goes a delicious assortment of biscuits, which we call cookies. Here is one.*

½ cup molasses
½ cup butter
1 scant cup flour

⅔ cup sugar
1 cup chopped walnuts

*Heat oven to 300°.*
*Grease baking sheet.*
*Heat molasses to boiling point. Add butter. Slowly stirring, constantly, add flour mixed and sifted with the sugar. Add nuts.*
*Drop from spoon, 2" apart, onto greased baking sheet. Bake in a 300° oven for 15 minutes. Cool slightly. Roll over handle of wooden spoon while warm.* Yield: approx. 4 dozen.

# FRANCE

## Lace Cookies

*The French are known world wide for their culinary arts. Add these gems to your cookie jar.*

1 cup flour
1 cup finely chopped nuts
½ cup corn syrup

½ cup shortening
⅔ cup packed brown sugar

*Heat oven to 375°.*
*Lightly grease baking sheet.*
*Blend flour and nuts. Bring corn syrup, shortening, and sugar to a boil in a saucepan over medium heat. Stir constantly. Remove from heat. Stir in flour and nuts.*
*Drop batter by level teaspoon 3″ apart on baking sheet, making 8–9 cookies at a time. Bake in a 375° oven for 5–6 minutes. Remove from oven. Allow to stand for 5 minutes. Remove from sheet.* Yield: 4 dozen.

## Cat's Tongue Cookies

9 tablespoons soft sweet butter
10 tablespoons sugar
3 egg whites

1½ cups sifted flour
1½ teaspoons vanilla

*Heat oven to 400°.*
*Grease baking sheet.*
*Cream butter and sugar. Add unbeaten egg whites, one by one, stirring well after each addition. Resift flour into mixture. Add vanilla. Mix.*
*Use a pastry tube fitted with a small plain tip. Force 3″ strips onto a greased baking sheet, leaving space between each strip.*
*Bake in a 400° oven for 6–8 minutes, until cookies are lightly browned around the edges.* Yield: 50–60 pieces.

# GERMANY

## Springerle

*A famous recipe made with traditionally designed, hand-carved rolling pins that are made especially for it.*

2 eggs
1 cup sugar

¼ teaspoon anise extract
1½ cups sifted flour

*Heat oven to 300°.*
*Grease and flour baking sheet.*
*Beat eggs and sugar in top of double boiler for 10 minutes (over hot water, not boiling). Remove from heat and beat until cool. Add anise. Fold in flour. Dough should be moderately stiff.*

*Place dough on floured board and sprinkle top generously with flour. Roll into ¼" thickness. Press design into dough with springerle rolling pin. Brush off excess flour.*

*Cut dough. Place on sheet and bake at 300° for 10 minutes. Turn heat off, keeping cookies in oven for another 5 minutes. Cool on rack.* Yield: 5 dozen.

## Pfeffernüsse

*Traditionally served at Christmas in German homes.*

3 eggs
1 cup sugar
3 cups flour
⅛ teaspoon cloves
¼ cup ground, blanched almonds

½ cup chopped candied orange
rind (4-ounce package)
¼ teaspoon baking powder
¼ teaspoon salt
⅛ teaspoon white pepper
1 teaspoon cinnamon

*Heat oven to 350°.*
*Grease baking sheet.*
*Beat eggs and sugar until frothy. Blend dry ingredients. Stir in. Add almonds and orange rind. Mix with hands. Roll dough ¼" thick on lightly floured board. Cut in 1" rounds. Place on lightly greased baking sheet and cover with towel. Leave overnight. (Bake immediately for a softer cookie.)*

*Bake in a 350° oven for 20 minutes, until lightly browned.* Yield: 12 dozen.

# GHANA

## Atsyomo

*My daughter's class made these twisted cakes for a parents' party.
I could hardly fight my way to the table for a second helping!*

1 egg
2 tablespoons sugar
¼ teaspoon nutmeg
¼ teaspoon aniseed
1 cup flour
½ teaspoon salt

¼ teaspoon baking powder
½ tablespoon melted margarine
¼ cup milk
Salad oil for deep frying
Sugar

*Beat egg in deep bowl. Add sugar, nutmeg, and aniseed. Beat.
Sift flour, salt, and baking powder. Stir into egg mixture. Add margarine and milk. Knead.*

*With a floured rolling pin roll out on a floured board to about
¼" thickness. Cut in 1" strips. Then cut into diamond shapes. Fry in
deep hot oil until golden brown. Drain on paper. Roll in sugar.*
Yield: 6 dozen.

# HAWAII

## Honolulu Lulus

*Close your eyes, bite into one of these . . . you're in Hawaii!*

½ cup light corn syrup
¼ cup butter
¼ cup shortening
⅔ cup brown sugar
1 cup sifted flour

¼ teaspoon salt
1 cup chopped walnuts
¾ cup flaked coconut
⅓ cup drained crushed pineapple

*Heat oven to 325°.*
*Grease baking sheet.*
*Mix and cook corn syrup, butter, shortening, and brown sugar in
saucepan. Stir often, until mixture comes to full boil.*
*Remove from heat. Blend in flour and salt. Fold in nuts, coconut,
and pineapple. Drop by teaspoon 3" apart on greased baking sheet.*

*Bake one sheet at a time in a 325° oven for 10–12 minutes. Cookies will be shiny at edges and beginning to brown.*

*Cool until slightly firm (1 minute). Lift from sheet to cooling rack with spatula.* Yield: 60 cookies.

## HOLLAND

### Cheese Wafers

*Leave it to the bakers of Holland to come up with this delicious use of cheese.*

| | |
|---|---|
| 1 (3 ounce) package cream cheese | 1 cup flour |
| ½ cup butter | Dried peaches or apricots |
| ½ cup sugar | Milk |
| | Sugar |

*Heat oven to 350°.*
*Grease baking sheet.*
*Blend cheese, butter, sugar, and flour. Shape in rolls 1" in diameter. Wrap in waxed paper. Chill overnight.*

*Slice rolls thin. Place slice of dried fruit on one slice of dough and cover with another slice of dough. Press edges together. Brush top with milk. Sprinkle with sugar.*

*Bake in a 350° oven for about 7 minutes.* Yield: 40 wafers.

## ITALY

### Spumette

*Pretty as a picture, and delicious, too, these pink meringues add color to your cookie plate.*

4 egg whites
1 cup powdered sugar
2 drops red vegetable coloring

*Heat oven to 375°.*
*Grease baking sheet.*
*Beat egg whites until frothy. Sift sugar and add to egg whites gradually. Beat until well blended. Add coloring and beat until stiff.*

*Drop by teaspoonful onto baking sheet, spacing 1" apart. Bake in a 375° oven for 10 minutes, until puffy and firm. Remove from oven. Cool. Remove from pan with spatula. Yield: 1½ dozen.*

## Apricot Cookies

*Another taste treat from Italy.*

¼ pound butter
½ cup sugar
3 tablespoons cream
1 egg

2 tablespoons apricot jam
1 cup flour
1 teaspoon baking powder

*Heat oven to 375°.*
*Grease baking sheet.*
*Cream butter, sugar, cream, egg, and jam. Sift flour and baking powder into mixture. Mix gently until flour is absorbed.*
*Drop by teaspoonfuls, about 1" apart, on greased baking sheet. Bake in a 375° oven for about 15 minutes, until light brown. Yield: 1½ dozen.*

# MEXICO

## Naquis

*Mexican food is usually "hot," but don't worry about these miniature doughnuts. They'll suit anyone's taste.*

1 egg
½ cup sugar
Pinch baking soda
½ teaspoon salt

⅓ cup buttermilk
2 cups sifted flour
Fat for deep frying

*Mix together all ingredients except fat, forming a soft dough. Add more milk if necessary. Roll and shape by hand into tiny doughnuts.*
*Fry in hot deep fat (350°). Drain on brown paper. Yield: 3 dozen.*

## Panecillos

*These are tasty round cookies.*

2 cups sifted flour
½ cup sugar
1 egg
1 tablespoon lemon juice

¼ cup olive oil
¼ cup chopped seedless raisins
½ cup chopped pecans
Additional sugar

*Heat oven to 350°.*
*Grease baking sheet.*

*Mix together flour, sugar, egg, lemon juice, olive oil, and chopped raisins to form a smooth dough. Mold into walnut-sized balls. Place on greased baking sheet. Sprinkle with pecans and additional sugar. Bake in a 350° oven for 20–25 minutes.* Yield: 3 dozen.

# NORWAY

## Berlinerkrauser

*Although a Norwegian cookie, the name means a cookie native to the Berlin area of Germany. Originally this recipe must have come from there and become an old Norwegian standby.*

1½ cups shortening (half butter
or margarine)
1 cup sugar
2 teaspoons grated orange rind
2 eggs

4 cups flour
1 egg white
2 tablespoons sugar
Red candied cherries
Green citron

*Heat oven to 400°.*

*Mix shortening, sugar, rind, and eggs. Sift in flour. Stir. Chill dough.*

*Break off small bits of dough. Roll to pencil size (6" long, ¼" thick). Form each piece into a circle. Bring one end over the other and through in a knot. Leave ½" end on each side of knot. Place on ungreased baking sheet.*

*Beat egg white until frothy; gradually beat in 2 tablespoons sugar. Brush tops with this mixture. Press bits of red cherries in center of knot. Add leaves of green citron.*

*Bake in a 400° oven for 10–12 minutes, until set, not brown.* Yield: 6 dozen 2" cookies.

## POLAND

### Filled Tea Thins

*Now here's a cookie delight for the eye and the palate.*

| | |
|---|---|
| 1 cup butter | ¼ teaspoon salt |
| ½ cup sugar | 1 cup chopped nuts |
| ¼ teaspoon vanilla extract | 1 cup raspberry jam |
| 2 cups sifted flour | Confectioners' sugar |

*Heat oven to 375°.*

*Cream butter, then blend in sugar, vanilla, flour, and salt. Add nuts. Roll on lightly floured board as thin as possible. Cut in small rounds. Bake in a 375° oven for 8–10 minutes.*

*When cooled, make sandwich of cookies by spreading bottom one with jam, then topping it with another cookie. Dust with confectioners' sugar.* Yield: 2 dozen.

## PORTUGAL

### Suspiros

*Maybe they named these cookies "sighs" because they were good beyond words!*

| | |
|---|---|
| ¾ cup chopped almonds | Pinch salt |
| ½ cup confectioners' sugar | 1 egg white |

*Heat oven to 350°.*

*Grease and flour baking sheet.*

*Mix almonds and sugar. Add salt to egg white and beat until stiff. Combine almond and egg mixture.*

*Drop from teaspoon 1" apart on baking sheet. Bake in a 350° oven for 15 minutes, until lightly browned.* Yield: 1 dozen.

## RUSSIA

### Tea Cakes

*Russians are famous tea drinkers too, and of course there are delicious cookies to go with the tea.*

1 cup butter
½ cup sifted confectioners' sugar
1 teaspoon vanilla extract
2½ cups flour

¼ teaspoon salt
¾ cup finely chopped nuts
Additional confectioners' sugar

*Heat oven to 400°.*

*Mix butter, sugar, and vanilla. Sift in flour and salt. Blend. Mix in nuts. Chill dough.*

*Roll dough in 1" balls. Place on ungreased baking sheet. Bake in a 400° oven for 10–12 minutes until set, not browned.*

*While warm, roll in confectioners' sugar. Cool. Roll in sugar again.* Yield: 4 dozen.

## SCOTLAND

### Chewy Teas

*They do wonderful things with oatmeal in Scotland!*

½ cup butter
1 cup brown sugar
2 cups quick-cooking rolled oats

¼ teaspoon salt
1 teaspoon baking powder

*Heat oven to 350°.*

*Grease 8" by 8" by 2" pan.*

*Mix butter and sugar in saucepan. Cook and stir until butter melts. Stir in remaining ingredients. Mix.*

*Pour into pan. Bake in a 350° oven for 20–25 minutes. Cool. Cut into bars.* Yield: 2 dozen bars.

Plate II.   Cookies to serve and send.
*The Nestlé Company, Inc.*

# SOUTH AMERICAN INDIANS

## Jumanas

*Something a little different.*

⅔ cup butter
1 cup sugar
2 eggs
1 teaspoon vanilla extract
½ cup sour cream
2¾ cups flour

1 teaspoon soda
½ teaspoon salt
½ teaspoon nutmeg
Green food coloring
Raisins or nuts

*Heat oven to 375°.*
*Lightly grease baking sheet.*
*Mix butter, sugar, eggs, and vanilla until fluffy. Stir in sour cream. In another bowl blend dry ingredients, stir into butter mixture. Add coloring.*
*Drop dough by teaspoonful onto sheet. Press nut or raisin into center of each cookie. Bake in a 375° oven for 8–10 minutes, until lightly browned.* Yield: 6 dozen.

# SWEDEN

## Rosenmunnar

*Cookies are an integral part of teatime in Sweden. The assortment is huge. "Red lips" are favorite cookies because of their attractiveness and taste.*

½ pound butter
½ cup sugar

2 cups sifted flour
Red jam

*Heat oven to 375°.*
*Cream butter and sugar till fluffy. Add flour. Shape in olive-sized balls. Press center down and fill with jam. Bake in a 375° oven for 15–20 minutes, until delicately browned around edges.* Yield: 65–75.

## Spritz

*These are traditional cookies at Christmas in Sweden.*

1 cup butter
⅔ cup sugar
3 egg yolks

1 teaspoon almond extract
2½ cups flour

*Heat oven to 400°.*
*Mix butter, sugar, egg yolks, and almond extract flavoring. Sift in flour. Work in flour. Use ¼ of dough at a time, forcing through a variety of cookie-press disks onto an ungreased sheet. Use different cookie-press disks for variety in shape (star, Christmas tree, wreath, bell, etc.).*
*Bake in a 400° oven for 7–10 minutes, until set, not browned.* Yield: 6 dozen.

## Oatmeal Cookies

⅔ cup butter
½ cup sugar
3 cups rolled oats, uncooked

1 egg, beaten
1 teaspoon almond extract

*Heat oven to 325°.*
*Put 1 teaspoon butter aside to grease baking sheet.*
*Knead butter, sugar, and oats with fingers into a solid mass. Blend. Add egg and almond extract. Mix.*
*Form marble-sized balls and place on baking sheet. Mash each cookie with fork tines. Bake in a 325° oven for 10–15 minutes, till golden brown.* Yield: 2½ dozen.

## Pepparkakor

*These are thin crisp ginger cookies, traditional at Christmas in Sweden. They are often hung on wooden trees as decoration.*

3 cups sifted flour
1 tablespoon ground ginger
2 teaspoons cinnamon
1 teaspoon cloves
½ teaspoon allspice
½ teaspoon nutmeg

1 teaspoon baking soda
1 cup butter
1 cup sugar
½ cup light molasses
1 egg
Decorator frosting (given below)

*Heat oven to 350°.*

*Lightly grease baking sheets.*

*Sift flour, ginger, cinnamon, cloves, allspice, nutmeg, and baking soda together. Cream butter and gradually add sugar, beating until fluffy. Add molasses and egg. Beat well. Add flour mixture gradually, beating until blended. Wrap in waxed paper and chill overnight.*

*Roll out dough, a small amount at a time, on a floured board. Cut with floured cutters of different shapes.*

*Place 2″ apart on lightly greased baking sheets. Bake in a 350° oven for 8–10 minutes, until lightly browned. Cool on wire rack. Design cooled cookies with decorator frosting.* Yield: 8 dozen.

## Decorator Frosting

1 egg
¼ teaspoon cream of tartar

⅛ teaspoon salt
1¾ cups sifted confectioners' sugar

*Beat egg, cream of tartar, and salt until soft peaks form. Gradually beat in confectioners' sugar. Beat till stiff peaks form.*

# UNITED STATES: MODERN AMERICAN COOKIES

*With all the recipes from the old country at their fingertips, American women, with new products and quicker working equipment, have devised their own recipes. So for even more variety in your holiday cookie assortment, try some of the following.*

## Lollipop Cookies

½ cup soft shortening
1 cup sugar
1 teaspoon grated lemon rind
1 egg
2 tablespoons milk
2 cups flour

1 teaspoon baking powder
½ teaspoon salt
½ teaspoon soda
Box chocolate mint wafers
Popsicle sticks

*Heat oven to 400°.*
*Lightly grease baking sheet.*
*Mix shortening, sugar, and lemon rind in bowl. Blend in egg and milk. In another bowl stir together flour, baking powder, salt, and soda. Blend dry ingredients into shortening mixture.*

*Drop 6 teaspoons dough far apart on baking sheet; flatten lightly with fingers. Put a chocolate wafer on each cookie. Place one popsicle stick on each cookie, making the cookie look like a lollipop. Place another spoonful of dough on top of each cookie and flatten dough, sealing edges with fork tines.*

*Bake in a 400° oven for 8–10 minutes, until light golden brown. Cool on wire rack.* Yield: about 1½ dozen.

## Peppermint Kisses

2 egg whites
Dash of salt
⅛ teaspoon cream of tartar
½ teaspoon peppermint extract

¾ cup sugar
1 (6 ounce) package of semi-sweet chocolate bits

*Heat oven to 325°.*

*Beat egg whites, salt, cream of tartar, and peppermint extract until soft peaks form. Gradually add sugar. Beat to stiff peaks. Fold in chocolate bits.*

*Cover baking sheet with brown paper. Drop mixture from teaspoon onto paper. Bake in a 325° oven for 20–25 minutes. While slightly warm, remove from sheet.* Yield: 3 dozen.

## Apricot Tarts

½ cup butter
1 cup (4 ounces) grated American cheese
1⅓ cups sifted flour

2 tablespoons water
1 cup dried apricots
1 cup sugar

*Heat oven to 375°.*

*Cream butter and cheese. Blend in flour. Add water and mix. Chill for 4–5 hours.*

*Meanwhile cook apricots according to package directions. Drain and mash. Stir sugar into hot fruit, cook and stir until smooth. Cool.*

*Divide chilled dough in half. Roll each half to 10″ square. Cut 2½″ squares. Place 1 teaspoon apricot filling on each 2½″ square. Fold over diagonal corners and seal.*

*Bake on ungreased baking sheet in a 375° oven for 8–10 minutes.* Yield: 2½ dozen.

## Tinted Cookies

½ cup butter
1 cup sugar
2 eggs
2 tablespoons cream
1 teaspoon vanilla extract

2½ cups flour
½ teaspoon salt
¼ teaspoon soda
Food coloring

*Heat oven to 400°.*

*Mix butter, sugar, and eggs. Stir in cream and vanilla. Stir dry ingredients together. Blend in. Tint dough with coloring. Chill dough for 4–5 hours.*

*Roll dough, a little at a time, to ⅛″ thickness on a well-floured, cloth-covered board. Keep rest of dough chilled while working.*

*Cut cookies with cookie cutters in the shapes of Santa, tree, reindeer, wreath, etc. Place on ungreased baking sheet. Bake in a 400° oven for 6–8 minutes, until lightly browned. Let stand a minute before removing from sheet. Optional: decorate with icing or sprinkles, etc.* Yield: 4–5 dozen.

## Macaroons

3 egg whites
⅔ cup sugar
3 tablespoons flour

¼ teaspoon salt
2 cups grated coconut
1 teaspoon vanilla extract

*Heat oven to 325°.*
*Lightly grease baking sheet.*
*Beat the egg whites until stiff, gradually beating in the sugar. Sift flour and salt, and fold in with coconut and vanilla. Drop on sheet. Bake in a 325° oven for 15–20 minutes.* Yield: 3 dozen.

## Wine Drops

½ cup shortening
1¼ cups sugar
2 eggs
½ cup port wine
2¾ cups flour

¼ teaspoon salt
½ teaspoon baking soda
½ teaspoon baking powder
1 cup raisins
1 cup chopped nuts

*Heat oven to 375°.*
*Cream shortening and sugar in large bowl. Add eggs, one at a time. Beat after each addition. Blend in wine. Sift flour once. Add*

salt, soda, and baking powder to sifted flour and sift again. Blend sifted ingredients into batter. Mix. Add raisins and nuts. Mix.

Drop dough by teaspoon onto ungreased baking sheet. Bake in a 375° oven until lightly browned. Yield: 4 dozen.

### Nut Butter Balls

| | |
|---|---|
| 1 cup soft butter | 2 cups sifted flour |
| ½ cup confectioners' sugar | 2 cups chopped nuts |
| ½ teaspoon salt | ½ cup confectioners' sugar |
| 1 teaspoon almond extract | |

Heat oven to 350°.

Cream butter and ½ cup confectioners' sugar. Add salt, almond extract, flour, and nuts. Mix. Chill dough until easy to handle.

Shape dough with fingers into 1" thick balls or crescents. Place on ungreased baking sheet. Bake in a 350° oven for 15 minutes, until light brown. While still warm roll in remaining ½ cup confectioners' sugar. Yield: 5 dozen.

### Pineapple Drop Cookies

| | |
|---|---|
| ¾ cup butter | 1 teaspoon soda |
| 1 cup sugar | ½ teaspoon salt |
| 1 egg | Additional pineapple preserves |
| ¼ cup pineapple preserves | Bag of shelled walnuts |
| 2¼ cups flour | |

Heat oven to 375°.

Cream butter and sugar. Beat in egg and preserves. Sift dry ingredients together and add. Mix.

Drop from teaspoon 2" apart on ungreased baking sheet. Bake in a 375° oven for 10 minutes. Cool for 2 minutes. Top with pineapple preserves in center of cookie. Add a walnut half to top of preserves. Yield: 42 cookies.

## Chocolate Snowballs

2 cups sifted flour
½ teaspoon salt
¾ cup butter
½ cup sugar
2 teaspoons vanilla extract

1 egg
1 cup chopped nuts
1 cup chocolate bits
Confectioners' sugar

*Heat oven to 350°.*

*Sift flour and salt. Blend butter, sugar, and vanilla. Beat egg into creamed mixture. Blend dry ingredients, nuts, and chocolate bits into mixture.*

*Shape into 1″ balls. Place on ungreased baking sheet. Bake in a 350° oven for 15–20 minutes. Cool, then roll in confectioners' sugar.* Yield: 6 dozen.

## Kris Krinkly Tops

1 (6 ounce) package semisweet chocolate bits
1 (6 ounce) package butter-scotch-flavored bits
1¼ cups sugar
¾ cup soft butter

½ teaspoon salt
2 eggs
2 teaspoons grated orange rind
2½ cups sifted flour
3 teaspoons baking powder
½ cup sifted confectioners' sugar

*Heat oven to 375°.*

*Melt chocolate bits and butterscotch bits together in top of double boiler over hot, not boiling, water. Remove from heat. Blend in sugar, butter, and salt. Beat in eggs and orange rind. Sift together flour and baking powder, stir into bits mixture. Chill until firm. Shape into balls, using a rounded tablespoon for each.*

*Roll lightly in confectioners' sugar. Place 2″ apart on ungreased cookie sheets. Bake in a 375° oven for 12–15 minutes.* Yield: 3 dozen.

## Christmas Chocolate Honeys

½ cup shortening
¼ cup sugar
1 teaspoon cinnamon
1 teaspoon vanilla extract
1 egg
1½ cups sifted flour

1 teaspoon baking powder
½ teaspoon salt
¾ cup honey
1 (6 ounce) package semisweet
chocolate bits
Candied cherries and angelica

*Heat oven to 400°.*
*Grease 15" by 10" by 1" pan.*
*Cream together shortening, sugar, cinnamon, and vanilla. Beat in egg. Sift together flour, baking powder, and salt; add to creamed mixture alternately with honey. Stir in chocolate bits.*
*Spread in greased pan. With edge of knife mark dough into 3" by 1" sections. Make holly designs by laying pieces of cherry and angelica on center of each section; do not press into dough. Bake in a 400° oven for 10–12 minutes. Cool. Cut into 3" by 1" bars.* Yield: 50 bars.

## Choco-Nut Chews

1½ cups quick-cooking rolled
oats
1 (14 ounce) can sweetened
condensed milk
1 teaspoon vanilla extract
½ teaspoon salt

½ teaspoon cinnamon
¼ teaspoon nutmeg
1 (16 ounce) package semisweet
chocolate bits
½ cup chunk-style peanut butter
Fudge frosting (given below)

*Heat oven to 350°.*
*Grease 8" square pan.*
*Combine oats, condensed milk, vanilla, salt, cinnamon, and nutmeg in mixing bowl. Add chocolate bits and peanut butter; blend well. Spread in pan. Bake in a 350° oven for 25–30 minutes. Cool. Frost with fudge frosting. Cut into 1¼" squares.* Yield: 3 dozen.

### Fudge Frosting

½ cup semisweet chocolate bits
1½ tablespoons milk

1 teaspoon vanilla extract
⅓ cup chopped peanuts

*Melt chocolate bits with milk in top of double boiler over hot, not boiling, water. Remove from heat; stir in vanilla. Spread over cooled Choco-Nut Chews. Sprinkle with chopped peanuts. Cut as directed above.*

### Butterscotch Poinsettia Cookies

2 cups sifted confectioners' sugar
1 cup soft butter
2 eggs
2 teaspoons vanilla
3 cups sifted flour
1 teaspoon salt

1 cup flaked coconut
1 (6 ounce) package divided butterscotch-flavored bits
Granulated sugar
½ cup candied red cherries (cut 8 wedges from 1 cherry)

*Heat oven to 375°.*
*Lightly grease cookie sheets.*
*Cream together confectioners' sugar and butter. Add eggs and vanilla; beat well. Sift together flour and salt; add gradually. Add coconut and ¾ cup butterscotch bits; mix well. Chill until firm. Form into balls, using a rounded teaspoon for each.*
*Place on lightly greased cookie sheets. Flatten with bottom of glass that has been dipped in granulated sugar. Place a reserved butterscotch bit in the center of each cookie. Use cherry wedges to make poinsettia. Bake in a 375° oven for 12 minutes. Remove from cookie sheets and cool on racks. Yield: 5 dozen cookies.*

## QUICK AMERICAN RECIPES

*If you are looking for timesavers and still want to bake your own assortment of Christmas cookies, try these.*

### Quick Candy Canes

1 roll "Sugar Slice 'n' Bake" Cookies (bought in stores)
1 can white icing
Red food coloring

*Heat oven to 375°.*
*Slice cookies ⅛" thick. Roll each one on pastry board to thickness of a pencil. Shape into cane.*
*Bake on ungreased baking sheet in a 375° oven for 7–10 minutes. Cool for 1 minute before removing to rack.*
*Frost cookies when cool, alternating between plain white icing and icing colored by red food coloring. Yield: 3 dozen.*

### Quick Cookie Christmas Wreaths

1 roll "Sugar Slice 'n' Bake" Cookies (bought in stores)
Green-colored sugar
Red cinnamon candies

*Heat oven to 375°.*
*Slice roll into cookies ⅛" thick. Roll each slice on pastry board to pencil thickness. Twirl in green sugar. Shape into wreaths on ungreased baking sheet. Overlap ends slightly.*
*Bake in a 375° oven for 7–10 minutes. Add red candies for bow.* Yield: 3½ dozen.

### Instant Chip Cookies

1 package white cake mix      ¼ cup soft butter
1 cup water                   1 cup chocolate chips
2 egg whites                  ½ cup chopped walnuts

*Heat oven to 375°.*
*Lightly grease baking sheet.*
*Place half of cake mix in bowl. Add water, egg whites, butter. Blend. Add rest of cake mix. Beat smooth with wooden spoon. Blend in chocolate chips and nuts.*
*Drop dough by teaspoon onto sheet. Bake in a 375° oven for 12 minutes.* Yield: 4 dozen.

## AMERICAN NO-BAKE COOKIES

*For cookies with no baking at all, these are perfect.*

### Ting-a-Lings

2 (6 ounces each) packages semisweet chocolate bits
4 cups Cheerios

*Melt chocolate over hot water. Cool at room temperature. Gently mix in Cheerios. Drop by tablespoon onto waxed paper. Refrigerate to set (about 2 hours).* Yield: 42 clusters.

### Sherry Pecan Balls

3 cups ground vanilla wafers
1 cup ground pecans
1 cup confectioners' sugar
3 tablespoons light corn syrup
1¾ tablespoons cocoa
½ cup sherry wine
¼ cup sifted confectioners' sugar

*Blend wafers and pecans with 1 cup confectioners' sugar, syrup, cocoa, and wine. Mix.*
*Pinch off small pieces of dough and roll into marble-sized balls. Roll in sifted confectioners' sugar.* Yield: 3 dozen.

### Lemon Balls

1½ cups crumbled vanilla wafers
1½ cups sifted confectioners' sugar
2 tablespoons cocoa
½ cup finely chopped pecans
2 tablespoons light corn syrup
¼ cup bottled lemon juice
Tinted sugar

*Mix wafers, confectioners' sugar, cocoa, pecans, corn syrup, and lemon juice. Allow to stand for 30 minutes.*
*Form small balls of dough. Add more corn syrup if dry. Roll balls in tinted sugar. Chill.* Yield: 2½ dozen.

### Chocolate Yummies

1 (6 ounce) package semisweet chocolate bits
⅓ cup butter
16 large marshmallows
½ teaspoon vanilla
1 cup shredded coconut
2 cups rolled oats (quick-cooking)

*Melt chocolate bits, butter, and marshmallows in top of double boiler. Stir smooth. Remove from heat. Stir in vanilla, coconut, and oats. Mix.*
*Drop by teaspoon onto waxed paper. Refrigerate.* Yield: 3 dozen.

## Toasted Almond Balls

1 (6 ounce) package semisweet chocolate bits
1 (6 ounce) package butter-scotch-flavored bits
¾ cup sifted confectioners' sugar
½ cup sour cream
1½ teaspoons grated orange rind
¼ teaspoon salt
2 cups vanilla wafer crumbs
¾ cup chopped, toasted almonds

*Melt chocolate and butterscotch bits together over hot (not boiling) water; remove from heat. Add confectioners' sugar, sour cream, orange rind, and salt; mix well. Blend in vanilla wafer crumbs. Chill until firm enough to handle. Shape into 1" balls. Roll in chopped nuts. Store in tightly covered container. Yield: 5 dozen.*

# Chapter 9

# RECIPES FOR INTERNATIONAL CHRISTMAS CANDIES

Not surprisingly candymaking dates from very early days when ancient peoples discovered honey. Our first descriptions of candy-like forms come from Europe about six hundred years before Christ's birth. Shops in Rome sold sweetmeats to the wealthy people who could afford them.

Early sweets were sticky and sugary. They were made from dried fruits, nut meats, sesame seeds, and spices, which were mixed and held together with honey. They were cut in pieces, rolled in flour, chopped nuts, or sesame seeds to prevent them from sticking together. German gingerbread bakers sold them in their shops around 1470.

By the sixteenth century the kings of Europe were indulging in large, luxurious banquets. In order to outdo each other's efforts, confectioners were employed to concoct new sweets. The art of sweet making became reserved almost completely for nobility and remained so for many years.

After America was discovered, explorers of the sixteenth century brought sugar back to the Old World. Until this time honey was the only sweetening agent used. By 1519, Cortez had tasted cocoa, a royal drink served to him by the Aztec emperor Montezuma. The Spaniards did not care for its bitter taste, but when sugar was added to it, they found it most enjoyable and introduced it to Spain. It was well liked, but, as in the New World, it was reserved for the aristocracy.

During the seventeenth century, while the gingerbread bakers produced sweets for the wealthy, people in monasteries and apothecary shops began making and selling them to the public. They developed other confections using the new products vanilla, sugar, and cocoa.

But they had not yet found a way to make chocolate. Apothecary shops in the American colonies sold peppermint, horehound, and wintergreen candy drops. Stick candy was the first real candy in the colonies. Later molasses taffy and sugar plums (bonbons) became popular.

By the late seventeenth century confectioners were employed by grocers who had the right to bake cakes and make sweets for public sale. They became the chief sellers of candy along with gingerbread and sweetmeats. Finally the demand for candy grew so great that some confectioners began to specialize in producing only candy and sweets. They were called conditors.

As time went on, cinnamon and vanilla were added to cocoa to improve the flavor. Still cocoa was used only as a drink. But by 1876, Daniel Peter, of Switzerland, finally developed a chocolate suitable for eating. Sometime after, people started coating sweets with chocolate and the popularity of candy grew by leaps and bounds. The rest is history.

## TIPS IN CANDYMAKING

A large heavy saucepan and a candy thermometer are extremely helpful in successful candymaking. Although, of course, there are many delicious candies that do not require temperature readings.

If you are using a thermometer, remember to adjust temperatures on the thermometer for altitude. They should read as follows for the various stages.

## CANDYMAKING TESTS

| Stage | Temperature on Thermometer | Description of Test |
| --- | --- | --- |
| Thread | 230°–234° | 2″ thread spun by syrup when dropped from spoon. |
| Soft Ball | 234°–240° | When syrup is dropped into very cold water, it forms soft ball that flattens when removed from water. |

| Firm Ball | 244°–248° | When syrup is dropped into very cold water, it forms firm ball that does not flatten when removed from water. |
| Hard Ball | 250°–266° | When syrup is dropped into very cold water, it forms hard ball that is plastic yet holds its shape. |
| Soft Crack | 270°–290° | When syrup is dropped into very cold water, it separates into hard but not brittle threads. |
| Hard Crack | 300°–310° | When syrup is dropped into very cold water, it separates into hard, brittle threads. |

Candy is another holiday goodie that can be made ahead of time and stored for future use. Fortunately most candy freezes well. Be sure to wrap the candy box with aluminum foil or plastic wrap when you freeze it. When it is ready to use, thaw unopened in the package to prevent discoloring.

When freezing popcorn balls, wrap each separately in clear plastic. Place wrapped balls in a polyethylene bag and store in your freezer. When it is ready to use, thaw in the wrapper.

Fudge freezes easily by turning into a disposable aluminum foil pan immediately after beating. Then wrap tightly and freeze.

What country originated each variety of candy is hard to determine. But here are some recipes that are usually associated with particular countries.

## BELGIUM

### Pralines

2 cups sugar
1 cup brown sugar
½ cup milk
½ cup condensed milk

¼ cup butter
¼ teaspoon salt
3 cups broken pecans

*Butter baking sheet.*
*Mix sugars, milks, butter, and salt in heavy saucepan. Bring to*

*rolling boil slowly over medium heat. Add nuts. Continue boiling until candy reaches soft-ball stage. Remove from heat. Stir only to give mixture a creamy look. Spoon onto buttered baking sheet. Cool.* Yield: 6 dozen.

# ENGLAND

## Mint Wafers

*The perfect candy treat after a filling Christmas dinner.*

3 tablespoons butter
3 tablespoons milk
1 (14 ounce) package white
  creamy-type frosting mix

Several drops oil of peppermint
Food coloring of your choice

*Melt butter with milk in top of double boiler. Add frosting mix and stir till smooth.*

*Cook for 5 minutes over rapidly boiling water. Stir occasionally. Add peppermint. Add desired food coloring.*

*Drop from teaspoon onto waxed paper. Keep rest of candy over hot water while dropping wafers. Swirl tops of candy with teaspoon. Cool until firm.* Yield: 5 dozen.

# FRANCE

## Fondant

*This recipe needs no cooking.*

⅓ cup soft butter
⅓ cup light corn syrup
½ teaspoon salt

1 teaspoon vanilla extract
3½ cups sifted confectioners'
  sugar

*Blend all, kneading until blended. Shape as desired.* Yield: 1⅓ pounds.

## Mocha Logs

*A carry-over from the ancient Yule log custom.*

*Use fondant no-cooking recipe, adding 2 teaspoons instant coffee to it.*

*Shape into ½″ by 2″ rolls. Roll in chocolate sprinkles.* Yield: about 1⅓ pounds.

## Candied Violets

*If you like the exotic, this is it!*

1 cup hot water
2 cups sugar
4 cups violets (fresh, washed, drained, and stemmed)

*Combine water and sugar and stir until sugar is dissolved. Add flowers. Simmer over medium heat until syrup is at soft-ball stage (234° F. on candy thermometer). Gently stir flowers with wooden spoon.*

*Remove from stove. Keep stirring until syrup begins to crystallize and has consistency of coarse meal. Drain. Shake off excess sugar. Cool on waxed paper. Pack flowers into sterilized jars. They are good for eating or for decorating cakes, desserts, etc.*

# ITALY

## Torrone

*This is the famous Italian Christmas nougat.*

1 cup honey
2 egg whites
1 cup sugar
2 tablespoons water
1 pound shelled and blanched almonds
½ pound shelled and slightly toasted hazelnuts
1 teaspoon small pieces of candied orange peel
½ teaspoon grated lemon rind
3 sheets Ostia wafers

*Line 2 or 3 (6″ by 8″) loaf pans with Ostia, a very thin sheetlike unleavened wheat bread.*

*Place honey in top of double boiler over boiling water. Stir with a wooden spoon until honey is caramelized (about 1 hour). Beat egg whites till stiff. Slowly add to honey. Mix well. Mixture will be fluffy and white.*

*Combine sugar and water in saucepan. Let boil until caramelized, without stirring. Add sugar mix to honey mixture a little at a time. Mix well. Cook mixture a little longer. When a little dropped into cold water hardens, add nuts, peel, and rind. Mix well and quickly before candy hardens.*

*Pour mixture in pans on top of Ostia about 2" deep. Cover with more wafers. Cool for 20 minutes. Cut down center lengthwise into 2 long rectangular pieces.* Yield: 4–6 long pieces.

## MEXICO

### Pecan Candy

*Easy to make, good to eat.*

2 cups ground pecans
1 cup powdered sugar
2 stiffly beaten egg whites

*Heat oven to 350°.*
*Butter baking sheet.*
*Mix pecans and sugar. Add egg whites. Form small balls from mixture. Bake on buttered sheet in a 350° oven for 5 minutes.* Yield: 16 candies.

### Orange Candy

*A fudge-like candy with a different tang.*

3 cups sugar
¼ cup water
1 cup undiluted evaporated milk

Pinch salt
2 teaspoons grated orange rind
1 cup chopped walnuts

*Lightly butter 8" square pan.*
*Place 1 cup sugar into a heavy frying pan and stir over medium heat with a wooden spoon until sugar is melted and caramelized to golden brown color. Add water. Stir until sugar completely redissolves. Add rest of sugar, milk, and salt. Place over low heat. Stir until mixture begins to boil. Stirring frequently, cook till soft-ball stage (236° on candy thermometer).*

*Remove from heat. Cool to lukewarm. Do not stir. Add rind and nuts. Beat till candy loses gloss and holds shape when dropped from a spoon. Pour into buttered pan and cool till set and firm. Cut into small squares.* Yield: about 5 dozen.

# SCOTLAND

## Marzipan

*A favorite candy in Scotland at Christmas.*

¼ pound finely ground, blanched almonds
¼ pound confectioners' sugar

1 egg white, beaten
¼ teaspoon salt

*Mix all ingredients. Knead smooth. Paste can be softened with a very little amount of lemon juice if it is too stiff.*

*Let stand covered for 24 hours before using. When ready to use, form into desired shapes.* Yield: depends on size of desired shapes.


# UNITED STATES: EARLY AMERICAN

## Old-Fashioned Glazed Almonds

*This is an Early American favorite.*

1 cup almonds
1 cup water
1 cup sugar

*Heat water and sugar together until sugar is dissolved completely. Place nuts in mixture, not more than 12 at a time. Boil gently until tender. Remove with slotted spoon, one at a time. Drain on absorbent paper. Sprinkle more sugar over nuts, coating all sides. Dry in cool oven. Keep in closely covered metal container.* Yield: 1 cup almonds.

The following candy recipes are used, with slight variations, all over the world.

### Apple-on-a-Stick

*Always a favorite with children.*

1 cup molasses
1 cup sugar
1 teaspoon cider vinegar
⅓ teaspoon salt

¼ cup water
2 tablespoons butter
12 small apples
12 popsicle sticks

*Combine molasses, sugar, vinegar, salt, and water. Slowly cook, stirring constantly, to hard-ball stage (270°). Remove from heat. Add butter. Dip apples into syrup, covering all sides. Cool on waxed paper. Insert popsicle stick for holder.* Yield: 12 portions.

### Cashew Brittle

*My mother's favorite.*

1 cup sugar
1 cup salted whole cashew nuts

*Butter pan.*
*Melt sugar in a heavy skillet over low heat. Stir constantly until sugar is dissolved and golden brown. Remove from stove. Add nuts. Pour into buttered pan, making a thin sheet of candy.*
*When cool, break into irregular pieces.* Yield: ½ pound.

### Peanut Clusters

*Better make a lot. They go like hot cakes!*

1 (4 ounce) package chocolate
  pudding mix
1 cup sugar
½ cup evaporated milk

1 teaspoon butter
1 cup salted peanuts
1 teaspoon vanilla extract

*Mix pudding, sugar, milk, and butter in saucepan. Cook and stir over medium heat until mixture boils. Reduce heat and stir for 3 minutes.*
*Remove from heat. Stir nuts and vanilla in quickly. Beat until mixture thickens and begins to lose gloss.*
*Drop from teaspoon into clusters on waxed paper. Cool.* Yield: 2 dozen.

### Apricot-Apple Drops

*Something a little different to suck on.*

1 cup nonfat dry milk solids
½ cup confectioners' sugar

½ cup Junior Food Apricot-
Applesauce (bought in stores)
A little grated lemon rind

*Mix above together until smooth. Drop by teaspoon onto waxed paper. Let stand for 1 hour.* Yield: depends on size of drop.

### Coconut Wreaths

*A good-looking, chewy candy, and a favorite with children.*

2 (8 ounce) packages (5¼ cups) shredded coconut
1 (15 ounce) can (1⅓ cups) sweetened condensed milk

2 teaspoons vanilla extract
4 drops green food coloring
Red cinnamon candies

*Heat oven to 350°.*
*Grease cookie sheet.*
*Stir together coconut, milk, vanilla, and food coloring. Drop by rounded spoonfuls 2" apart onto a well-greased cookie sheet. With spoon shape into wreath. Trim with candies. Bake in a 350° oven for 8 minutes. Cool on rack.* Yield: 4½ dozen.

### Coconut Fruit Balls

1½ cups cooked and pitted prunes
1½ cups pitted dates
¾ cup dried apricots
½ cup raisins
1 cup walnuts

¼ cup sugar
¼ cup thawed concentrated orange juice
1 (3½ ounce) can flaked coconut

*Grind fruits and nuts coarsely. Add sugar and orange juice. Form into 1" balls and roll in coconut.* Yield: 10 dozen.

## Quick Caramel Popcorn Balls

*The kids love them.*

| | |
|---|---|
| 2 quarts popped corn | 2 tablespoons water |
| ½ pound (28) vanilla caramels | Dash salt |

*Keep popped corn hot in a 300° oven. Combine caramels and water in top of double boiler. Stir frequently. Add salt.*

*Place corn in large bowl. Pour sauce over. Toss corn until coated. Butter hands and shape coated corn into balls 1½" in diameter.* Yield: about 2 dozen small balls.

## Penuche

*A well-known old stand-by.*

| | |
|---|---|
| 4½ cups firmly packed light brown sugar | ¼ teaspoon salt |
| 1 cup undiluted evaporated milk | 1 teaspoon vanilla extract |
| ½ cup butter | 2 cups chopped walnuts |

*Mix sugar, milk, butter, and salt in a large saucepan. Cook and stir until sugar dissolves. Continue cooking until soft-ball stage (238° on candy thermometer).*

*Remove from stove. When lukewarm add vanilla and nuts. Beat until mixture is thick and loses gloss.*

*Pour into 9" square buttered pan. Cut into squares when firm.* Yield: 3 pounds.

## Divinity

*Always a favorite.*

| | |
|---|---|
| ½ cup light corn syrup | 2 egg whites, stiffly beaten |
| 2½ cups sugar | 1 teaspoon vanilla extract |
| ¼ teaspoon salt | 1 cup coarsely chopped nuts |
| ½ cup water | |

*Mix syrup, sugar, salt, and water in a saucepan. Cook and stir until sugar dissolves. Continue cooking, but don't stir, until firm-ball stage (248° on candy thermometer).*

*Pour half of syrup over egg whites; beat constantly. Cook remainder of syrup until soft-crack stage (272° on candy thermome-*

*ter). Add slowly to first mixture. Beat until holds shape. Add vanilla and nuts. Drop by teaspoon onto waxed paper. Cool.* Yield: 1½ pounds.

### Christmas Tree Candy

*Very attractive to serve.*

2 tablespoons confectioners' sugar
2 packages lime gelatin
6 cups flaked coconut
1¼ cups blanched almonds

1 (15 ounce) can sweetened condensed milk
1 tablespoon sugar
20–25 drops green food coloring
¼ teaspoon vanilla extract
Butter frosting (given below)

*Sift confectioners' sugar with 3 tablespoons gelatin and set aside. Finely grind coconut and almonds. Add milk, sugar, coloring, vanilla, and remaining gelatin. Mix. Form cone-like Christmas trees from the mix and roll them in confectioners' sugar mix.*

### Butter Frosting

1 tablespoon butter
½ cup sifted confectioners' sugar
1 teaspoon milk

*Cream butter. Gradually add ¼ cup sugar and blend. Add another ¼ cup sugar, alternating with the teaspoon milk until mixture becomes the right consistency to spread.*

*Frost base of trees with butter frosting. Chill until firm. Store in covered container at room temperature.* Yield: 10 dozen trees.

### Marshmallow Pecan Roll

*Delicious!*

1 (7½ ounce) jar marshmallow cream
3½ cups confectioners' sugar
1 teaspoon vanilla extract

¼ teaspoon almond extract
1 pound caramels
2½ pounds coarsely chopped pecans (10 cups)

*Combine marshmallow, sugar, and extracts. Gradually knead in the last of the sugar. Shape into 8 rolls (1" in diameter). Wrap in plastic wrap and put in freezer until candy is very hard.*

*Melt caramels in top of metal double boiler. Remove from heat but keep over hot water. Dip marshmallow rolls into caramel to cover. Roll in nuts. Press nuts into caramel with hands. Cool. Store in cool, dry place, covered.* Yield: 5 pounds.

### Easy Chocolate Fudge

*Melts in your mouth.*

½ cup butter
1 (4 ounce) package chocolate pudding mix
1 (3 or 3¼ ounce) package vanilla pudding mix

½ cup milk
1 (1 pound) box sifted confectioners' sugar
½ teaspoon vanilla extract
½ cup chopped walnuts

*Butter a 10″ by 6″ by 1½″ baking dish.*

*Melt butter in saucepan. Stir in dry puddings and milk. Bring to boil. Stirring constantly, boil for 1 minute.*

*Remove from heat. Beat in sugar. Stir in vanilla and nuts. Pour into buttered baking dish. Chill before cutting in 1½″ squares.* Yield: 24 squares.

### Caramel Turtles

*My favorite.*

1 cup small pecan halves
36 light caramels
½ cup melted semisweet chocolate bits

*Heat oven to 325°.*
*Grease cookie sheet.*
*Arrange pecans in groups of 4 like a star, flat side down on cookie sheet. Place one caramel on each cluster of pecans.*

*Heat in a 325° oven until caramels soften (4–8 minutes). Remove from oven. Flatten caramels over pecans with a buttered spatula. Cool slightly. Remove to waxed paper. Swirl melted chocolate over top to create turtles.* Yield: 36 turtles.

### Creamy Chocolate Bites

*If you want to gain weight, this will do it!*

1 package fudge-flavored frosting mix
½ cup soft butter
1 teaspoon vanilla extract

Hot water
Confectioners' sugar
1 cup chopped pecans or walnuts
or chocolate sprinkles

*Mix fudge frosting, butter, and vanilla and work with hands into a ball. Add a few drops hot water to make mix workable. Lightly dust board with confectioners' sugar and knead mixture on board 20 times.*

*Pinch off walnut-sized pieces of mixture and roll into ball shape. Then roll in nuts or chocolate sprinkles.* Yield: 48 balls.

### Chocolate-Covered Cherries

*This is another one of my favorites.*

1 (4 ounce) jar stemmed red maraschino cherries
1 (4 ounce) jar stemmed green maraschino cherries
1 (12 ounce) package chocolate fudge mix

*Drain cherries and dry thoroughly on paper towel. Prepare fudge mix as directed on package. Add more water if needed to make dipping easier.*

*Keep fudge in double boiler over hot water. Dip each cherry, leaving the top and stem of the cherry uncovered. Place dipped cherry on waxed paper and allow to set. Store covered in cool place.* Yield: 2½ dozen.

### Layered Filbert Truffles

*Who can resist these?*

3 cups finely chopped, toasted
filberts
3 cups sifted powdered sugar
1 egg white
¼ cup dark rum

1½ cups semisweet chocolate
bits
¾ cup sweetened condensed milk
1 tablespoon butter

*Butter an 8″ square pan.*

*Mix well nuts, sugar, egg white, and rum. Press mixture evenly and firmly into pan. Melt chocolate bits in top of double boiler over boiling water. Stir in milk and butter. Cook until thickened. Spread chocolate mixture over the layer of nuts in the pan. Let stand in cool place until firm. Cut into small squares.* Yield: 5 dozen.

## Marzipan Ornaments

*This candy is used to make ornaments for the tree, cake, gifts, or to eat. The ornaments will last about 2 weeks at room temperature and a month in the refrigerator . . . if they aren't eaten before!*

1 cup (5-ounce jar) marshmallow cream
⅓ cup light corn syrup
⅛ teaspoon salt
6 cups sifted powdered sugar
1 teaspoon vanilla extract

1 pound almond paste (available in most food specialty shops)
Vegetable colorings
Powdered sugar paint (given below)

*Mix marshmallow, corn syrup, salt, 2 cups powdered sugar, and the vanilla. Heat slowly to lukewarm. Crumble almond paste into the mixture. Keep warm and stir until blended.*

*Remove from heat. Sift remaining sugar onto pastry board. Spoon mixture into a mound of remaining powdered sugar and knead until the sugar is absorbed.*

*Divide the marzipan into portions. Tint each a different color. Shape to desired forms. After ornaments dry overnight, paint on designs or faces with powdered sugar paint.*

## Powdered Sugar Paint

*Mix powdered sugar with desired food coloring to a paste-like consistency. Then use as you would paints. Use watercolor type brush for painting.*

# Chapter 10

# RECIPES FOR INTERNATIONAL CHRISTMAS DRINKS

Since earliest times drinks and toasts have been with us. Even today Christmas without the usual punch bowl on the table and the round of toasts with family and friends doesn't seem much like Christmas. This is a time to drink to each other's health and to wish all good wishes with the glass held high. Some drinks are mild and mellow, others colorful and tempting, and still others, like *glögg* and *krupnik,* pack a punch.

Down through the ages special drinks have become associated with Christmas in different countries.

## AUSTRIA

### Spiced Viennese Coffee

*This one adds zip to the old cup of coffee!*

7 tablespoons instant coffee
7 whole cloves
2 ½" sticks cinnamon
7 cups boiling water

½ cup sugar
1 cup heavy cream, whipped
Cinnamon

*Place coffee, cloves, and sticks of cinnamon in a saucepan. Pour boiling water over them. Cover and bring to a boil. Remove from heat. Let stand for 5–8 minutes. Strain into preheated carafe. Add sugar. Stir until sugar dissolves. Serve immediately. Garnish each cup with whipped cream and a dash of cinnamon.* Yield: 8 servings.

# ENGLAND

## Hot Apple Toddy

*The original toddy was an Asian drink made of the fermented sap of a palm tree. British traders of the Far East brought the word and the drink into English use.*

1 quart apple juice  
⅓ cup brown sugar  

½ lemon, sliced  
Angostura Bitters  

*Mix juice, sugar and lemon in a saucepan. Bring to a boil. Simmer for 5 minutes. Add several dashes of Angostura Bitters. Serve warm.* Yield: 1 quart (6 servings).

## Lamb's Wool

*An old medieval drink.*

4 cups apple juice  
2 cups orange juice  
Cinnamon stick  
½ cup honey  

3 tablespoons lemon juice  
1 teaspoon grated orange rind  
Marshmallows  

*Simmer all together. Cool. Serve with marshmallow (the fluff of wool) floating on top.* Yield: 6 servings.

## Sillabub

*Syelabub was the original word for this drink. It came from: "sille," a kind of wine from the champagne district of Sillery, in France, and "bub," an Elizabethan slang word for bubbling drink.*

2 cups white wine  
½ cup lemon juice  
Grated rinds of 2 lemons  
1½ cups sugar  

1 quart milk  
4 egg whites  
Grated nutmeg  

*Combine wine, lemon juice, rinds, and 1 cup sugar. Stir until sugar dissolves. Add milk and beat till frothy. Beat eggs and add remaining ½ cup sugar to them, a little at a time. Float the stiff egg whites on top of the liquid in a punch bowl. Sprinkle top with nutmeg.* Yield: 10 6-ounce cups.

Plate III brings back heart-warming thoughts of Christmas, gatherings of family and friends before a roaring fire to partake of the punch bowl of sillabub and tempting desserts.

## Wassail

*The name is derived from the Middle English words Waes Haeil, the toast that meant "Be thou well."*

1 gallon sweet or hard cider
10  2" sticks cinnamon
1 tablespoon allspice

½ cup fresh lemon juice
2 cups sugar
1 bottle (fifth) applejack

*Heat all together except applejack, until mixture comes to a boil. Simmer for 15 minutes. Add applejack. Serve hot. Decorate bowl with baked apples if so desired.* Yield: 25 6-ounce cups.

# GERMANY

## German Punch

*A tasty combination.*

1 cup grape juice
1 cup cider
½ cup grapefruit juice

1 quart club soda
Sugar to taste

*Mix all ingredients. Pour into a punch bowl over a large cake of ice.* Yield: 7–8 cups.

# HONDURAS

## Hot Pineapple Punch

*A new taste treat.*

3 pineapples
3 cups water
3  2" cinnamon sticks
2 teaspoons whole cloves

2 teaspoons whole allspice
¾ cup sugar
1 cup coconut milk
1 quart light rum

*Peel and chop pineapple and add water. Let stand overnight. Put mixture into a large saucepan. Add spices, sugar, and milk. Boil for*

*5 minutes. Strain into a pitcher. Add rum. Serve hot.* Yield: 8–12 servings.

## ITALY

### Cappuccino

*Delicious!*

4 cups hot water
4 tablespoons instant cocoa mix

4 heaping teaspoons instant coffee
½ cup brandy or rum

*Mix above ingredients. Serve in demitasse cups.* Yield: 8–10 servings.

## MEXICO

### Mexican Hot Chocolate

*The Aztecs in Mexico used cacao beans as money as well as food. They also mixed it with cornmeal and herbs to make mush. But the Dutch, French, Italians, and Austrians experimented with the bean until they discovered a real drinking chocolate. Chocolate houses became the fashion, and people gathered in these places to drink chocolate, discuss politics, and gossip. Today the Mexicans use the bean for drinks such as this one.*

2 ounces unsweetened chocolate
3 tablespoons sugar
4 teaspoons crushed, toasted, blanched almonds

1 cup water
3 cups milk
Almond extract
⅛ teaspoon cinnamon

*Melt chocolate in the top of a double boiler. Add sugar and almonds. Gradually add water and milk. Simmer together for 10 minutes, then add almond extract and cinnamon. Beat until frothy.* Yield: 4 cups.

# POLAND

## Krupnik

*A hot grog with honey which goes to the feet and is said to fell the mighty and conquer the conquerors.*

1 cup dark honey
1 cup water
8 (1 ounce) cinnamon sticks
1 ½" piece crushed vanilla bean

¼ whole nutmeg, freshly grated
6 cloves, crushed
Freshly grated lemon rind
1 pint vodka

*Mix honey and water. Add remaining ingredients except vodka. Simmer for 10 minutes. Set in a warm place for 30 minutes. Strain through cheesecloth. Bring to a boil again. Pour immediately into a heated, covered pitcher. Add vodka and stir.*

*Serve in very hot liqueur glasses.* Yield: 1 quart.

# SWEDEN

## Glögg

*Always served at the Swedish Christmas party that is called Julkalas.*

2 bottles claret
12 blanched almonds
6 whole cardamom
2 2" sticks cinnamon
3 cloves
¼ cup raisins

¼ cup currants
10 dried apricots
1 pound lump sugar
1 quart aquavit or vodka
1 cup brandy
2 bottles port wine

*Simmer claret, almonds, cardamom, cinnamon, cloves, raisins, currants, and apricots for 1½ hours. Strain, keeping fruit and nuts. Pour liquid into a large punch bowl. Place a cake rack across the top of the bowl and arrange sugar lumps on it. Heat aquavit or vodka and brandy. Pour over sugar. Light it and let it blaze until the sugar melts and the flame dies. Remove the rack. Add heated port and the reserved fruits and nuts. Serve warm.* Yield: 5 quarts (30 servings).

# UNITED STATES

## Grape Fizz

*An old-fashioned drink popular in years gone by.*

1 quart ginger ale
1 quart grape juice

*Mix together and pour into glasses over crushed ice.* Yield: 8 servings.

## Southern Eggnog

*Very holiday-looking.*

1 package vanilla pudding and pie-filling mix
½ cup sugar
1 quart milk
3 egg yolks, slightly beaten
3 egg whites
1 teaspoon vanilla extract (or peach brandy)
¼ cup Grand Marnier
1 cup heavy cream
Nutmeg

*Mix pudding, sugar, and ¼ cup milk in a 2-quart saucepan. Add egg yolks. Blend. Add remaining milk. Mix well. Cook over medium heat. Stir constantly until mixture comes to a full boil. Cool.*

*Beat egg whites until stiff peaks form. Fold into cool pudding. Add vanilla (or brandy) and Grand Marnier. Chill for several hours.*

*Whip cream and spoon into eggnog just before serving. Sprinkle top with nutmeg.* Yield: 12 servings.

Other drinks associated with Christmas and holiday time are made, with variations, in many countries of the world. Here are some recipes for them.

Plate III.  A Very Merry Christmas and a Glad New Year!
*Courtesy of General Foods Corp.*

## Bubbling Jade Punch

*A spectacular-looking punch.*

1 package lime gelatin
1 cup hot water
2 cups cold water
1 (6 ounce) can frozen
    concentrated lemonade

1 cup pineapple juice
1 bottle champagne
Whole fresh strawberries

*Dissolve gelatin in hot water. Add cold water, concentrated lemonade, pineapple juice; blend. Add champagne, strawberries, and ice before serving.* Yield: 15–20 4-ounce cups.

## Electric Punch

*A colorful psychedelic-looking drink.*

2 (10 ounce) packages frozen
    raspberries
⅔ cup sugar
⅔ cup orange juice

1 (6 ounce) can frozen concentrated lemonade
1 quart ginger ale

*Thaw berries, then sprinkle with sugar. Add orange juice and reconstituted lemonade. When serving, pour fruit mixture over ice and add the ginger ale.* Yield: 2½ quarts.

## Fruit Punch

*A festive-looking punch for the youngsters and teetotalers.*

1 can Heart's Delight Juici-
    Drink (46 fluid ounces)
1 quart ginger ale

2 pints orange sherbet
Ice cubes with cherries frozen in
    them

*Mix juice and ginger ale in punch bowl. Add balls of sherbet. Add ice cubes.* Yield: 2½ quarts.

### Hot Spiced Cranberry Punch

*Very Christmas-looking drink.*

| | |
|---|---|
| 1 quart cranberries | 10 cloves |
| 1 quart water | ½ lemon, thinly sliced |
| ¾ cup sugar | 2 cups hot tea |
| 2 2" cinnamon sticks | |

*Cook cranberries in water until the skins pop open. Without stirring or pressing, strain through cheesecloth. Add sugar to strained juice. Tie cinnamon sticks and cloves in a cheesecloth bag and place bag in the cranberry juice and simmer for 5 minutes.*

*Add lemon and tea. Remove spice bag. Serve hot.* Yield: 8 servings.

### Hot Spicy Punch

*Very tasty.*

| | |
|---|---|
| 1 quart cider or dry red wine | 1 teaspoon whole cloves |
| 1 cup orange juice | 2 tablespoons chopped |
| ½ cup lemon juice | crystallized ginger |
| 2 2" cinnamon sticks | Light brown sugar to taste |

*Bring all ingredients except sugar to a boil. Simmer for 15 minutes. Preheat bowl. Strain ingredients through cheesecloth into the bowl. Add sugar to taste. Serve hot.* Yield: 8 servings.

### Punch Delight

*Attractive drink. Tasty for the children.*

| | |
|---|---|
| 1 (6 ounce) can frozen concentrated tangerine juice, thawed | 6 cups water |
| 1 (6 ounce) can frozen concentrated lemonade, thawed | 1 package frozen strawberries, thawed |
| 1 (6 ounce) can frozen concentrated orange juice, thawed | 1 quart cold ginger ale |

*The day before, mix tangerine juice with 1½ cups water. Put in freezer tray. Freeze into cubes.*

*The day of serving, mix lemonade and orange concentrates with 4½ cups water in a chilled punch bowl. Put in tangerine cubes and 1 tray plain ice cubes. Add strawberries and chilled ginger ale.* Yield: 3 quarts (15 servings).

## Orange Blossom Milk Punch

*Children like this.*

4 cups cold milk
4 cups cold orange juice
Sugar to taste

Orange slices
Maraschino cherries
Bamboo skewers

*Combine milk and juice in a shaker. Shake until thoroughly blended. Add sugar to taste. Pour into chilled glasses. Thread orange slices and cherries onto bamboo skewers. Place 1 in each glass.* Yield: 6–8 servings.

## Eggnog

*A very smooth Christmasy-looking drink.*

1 dozen eggs, separated
¾ cup sugar
1 pint bourbon or rye whiskey

1 quart cream
Brandy (optional)

*Beat egg yolks slightly and gradually add sugar, beating constantly. Add whiskey, a few drops at a time at first. Beat and add cream while beating. Fold in whipped egg whites. Add a small amount of brandy to taste. Mixture should be thick.* Yield: 2½ quarts (20 servings).

## Orange Eggnog

*Something a little different.*

6 eggs, separated
1 (6 ounce) can frozen concentrated orange juice, thawed
Juice of 1 lemon

½ teaspoon nutmeg
5 cups milk
½ cup sugar

*Beat egg yolks until foamy. Slowly add juices, nutmeg, and milk. Beat egg whites stiff. Slowly add sugar. Fold into egg yolk mixture.* Yield: 8–10 servings.

## Mulled Cider

*Always popular down through the years.*

2 quarts cider
1 orange, sliced
1 lemon, sliced
4 sticks cinnamon

6 whole cloves
¼ teaspoon nutmeg
¼ teaspoon ginger
Cinnamon sticks to garnish

*Simmer all ingredients in a saucepan over low heat for ½ hour. Serve hot. Add a stick of cinnamon to each serving for garnish.* Yield: 10 servings.

## Orange Rum Shrub

*A tasty combination.*

1 pound sugar
1 quart orange juice
2 quarts rum

Orange peel
Shaved ice

*Dissolve sugar in the orange juice. Add rum. Mix well, cover, and let stand for 3–4 weeks. Strain and bottle.*

*The flavor of orange peel may be added by soaking a few peelings in the rum for 12 hours.*

*To serve, pour into tall glasses over shaved ice.* Yield: 15 glasses.

## Coffee Sparkle

*Tasty and attractive drink.*

3 cups double-strength coffee
½ teaspoon vanilla extract
Sugar

Sparkling water
Frozen whipped cream
Grated chocolate

*Cool coffee. Combine with vanilla and sugar. Pour into goblets and fill glasses with sparkling water. Top with frozen whipped cream. Sprinkle grated chocolate over topping.* Yield: 4 servings.

## Maple Milkshake

*For the younger set.*

3 cups hot milk
6 marshmallows, cut up
4–6 teaspoons maple syrup

2 tablespoons malted milk
powder
Marshmallows for garnish

*Beat all ingredients except garnish together. Chill and float a marshmallow on top of each serving.* Yield: 4 servings.

## Strawberry Velvet

*Lovely to look at.*

4 cups cold milk
1 cup puréed sweetened
strawberries

Chilled whipped cream
4 whole strawberries

*Combine milk and strawberries in a shaker. Shake until thoroughly blended. Pour into glasses. Garnish each serving with whipped cream topped with a strawberry.* Yield: 4 servings.

# Chapter 11

# RECIPES FOR CHRISTMAS PRESERVES

All over the world preserves have always been favorites, not only to sweeten foods for everyday eating, but to add that extra touch at holidays and celebrations. In the old days a gift of preserves from a friend's kitchen was a special Christmas treat.

Recipes from all over the world found their way to the United States with the immigrants, and today we call them "our own." They are delicious on breads, crackers, with meats, fowl, or game.

## TIPS ON PRESERVING

*Jelly glasses:* Screw-on lids are best; otherwise get ones with metal lids to keep out ants and other insects.

Before using the glasses always wash and sterilize all glasses and lids and keep them warm when pouring jelly.

*Paraffin seal:* When ready to seal preserves, melt paraffin in the top of a double boiler or over a pan of water, *never directly over a flame.*

For preserving leave ½″ space at the top of the jelly glass. Wipe this space dry, then fill the space half full with wax while the preserve is hot. After cooling, the remaining space may be filled with wax for final sealing. Then add the lid.

To make the jars airtight, dip the end of the container, with the lid in place, into melted wax to seal all openings.

# TIPS ON DECORATING JELLY GLASSES

Nothing is as attractive as decorating the jelly glass or jar with your own especially designed personal label. You can draw a picture on the label if you are talented, or paste a colored magazine picture of a Christmas scene or the front of an old Christmas card on the jar to make it festive-looking. Or you can simply put a label stating, "From the kitchen of . . ." or "Made for you by . . ."

Topped with a colorful bow, wool pompon, or sprig of greenery, it makes a lovely and much-appreciated gift.

## JAMS

### Strawberry

*This French recipe is great on cream cheese and crackers, or as a topping on ice cream.*

5½ cups washed and dried strawberries
5 cups sugar
½ cup lemon juice

*Place berries in a wide, shallow pan, add the sugar, heat slowly. Increase the heat when the sugar is dissolved and bring to a boil slowly. Boil for 10 minutes.*

*Add lemon juice and continue to boil for exactly 2 minutes more. Spoon into glasses. Add paraffin seals and lids. Yield: 7 6-ounce glasses.*

### Banana

*This recipe, originally from India, makes a real gift treat. Not only is it delicious on muffins, but it makes an excellent filling between the layers of white cake.*

3 medium lemons
3 cups sugar
3 cups water

8 medium-sized, ripe bananas, mashed
1 whole piece dried green ginger
A few cloves

*Squeeze lemons. Cut rind to paper-thin slices. Boil sugar and wa-*

*ter for 10 minutes. Add lemon juice, rind, and mashed bananas, ginger, and cloves. Cook slowly for ½ to ¾ of an hour, stirring to prevent scorching. It is ready when it becomes a pale yellow mush.*

*Take out the piece of ginger. Pour into glasses. Add paraffin seals and lids.* Yield: 7 8-ounce glasses.

### Damson Plum

*Excellent for those who enjoy a tart jam at breakfast or with roasted meats. This Scottish recipe is really a good one.*

1 quart washed and stemmed damson plums
2 cups sugar

¼ cup orange juice
¼ cup water

*Combine ingredients and bring to a boil. Simmer slowly until desired thickness. (Use Chilled Plate Test, given below.) Remove from stove. Remove pits.*

*Pour into glasses. Add paraffin seals and lids.* Yield: 3 8-ounce glasses.

### Chilled Plate Test

*Put a teaspoon of boiling jam on a chilled plate. Place in the refrigerator for fast cooling. If runny when cool, simmer a while longer, then test again for desired thickness.*

### Beach Plum

*Here is a real native American jam enjoyed by the early colonists. Beach plums are still free for the picking at Cape Cod and on the Maine shores, making a delicious tart jam.*

4 cups washed and pitted beach plums
2 tablespoons water
4 cups sugar

*Simmer plums and water in a covered pot until the fruit is soft. Press them through a sieve. Add sugar. Cook until fruit is transparent. Stir constantly. Pour into glasses. Add paraffin seals and lids.* Yield: about 6 8-ounce glasses.

## Peach

*To keep that delicious summer peach taste on hand all year round, try this recipe.*

6 peaches, peeled, pitted, and halved
2 navel oranges, quartered

½ lemon, cut in two
Sugar to measure

*Grind fruits with medium blade of food chopper. Measure. Add an equal measure of sugar. Stir. Allow to stand overnight.*

*Boil for 20 minutes. Pour into glasses. Add paraffin seals and lids.* Yield: 5 8-ounce glasses.

## Pineapple-Strawberry

*These combined flavors will make this a much-sought-after gift.*

1 package frozen strawberries, thawed
1 (1 pound 4 ounce) can crushed pineapple

¼ cup water
1 package powdered fruit pectin
3½ cups sugar

*Measure 1 cup strawberries and juice into a large saucepan. Add pineapple, water, and pectin. Mix. Stirring constantly, bring to a boil. Add sugar and bring to rolling boil again. Boil for 1 minute.*

*Remove from heat. Stir and skim by turns for 5 minutes. Spoon into glasses. Add paraffin seals and lids.* Yield: 7 6-ounce glasses.

## Plum-Nut

*For those who like a chewy jam.*

½ lemon
2 oranges
3 pounds plums

3 pounds sugar
1 pound currants
½ pound chopped black walnuts

*Grind lemon and oranges. Quarter and pit plums, add to lemon and oranges. Add sugar and currants. Simmer for about 1½ hours. Add nuts. Cook for about 45 minutes more.*

*Spoon into glasses. Add paraffin seals and lids.* Yield: 12 8-ounce glasses.

## Spiced Blueberry

*A twofold gift. Mildly spiced for breakfast toast, also delicious as relish with fowl or game.*

| | |
|---|---|
| 1 quart stemmed and washed blueberries | ¼ teaspoon allspice |
| | ¼ teaspoon cinnamon |
| ¼ cup cider vinegar | ⅛ teaspoon cloves |
| 2 cups sugar | |

*Simmer all ingredients together until jam is desired thickness and blueberry skins are tender. (Use Chilled Plate Test, see Index.)*

*Pour into glasses. Add paraffin seals and lids.* Yield: 4 8-ounce glasses.

## Spiced Cherry

*Tart and tasty.*

| | |
|---|---|
| 5 cups pitted cherries | ½ teaspoon ground cinnamon |
| 4 cups sugar | ¼ teaspoon ground allspice |
| 1 cup cider vinegar | ¼ teaspoon ground cloves |

*Boil sugar, vinegar, cinnamon, allspice, and cloves together. Add cherries. Cook until jam is thick. (Use Chilled Plate Test.)*

*Pour into glasses. Add paraffin seals and lids.* Yield: 5 8-ounce glasses.

# JELLIES

### Mulberry Malinova

*A Czechoslovakian jelly that is a different taste treat.*

1 quart freshly squeezed, strained raw mulberry juice
¾ cup sugar
1 quart ginger ale

*To obtain mulberry juice, put berries in cheesecloth and squeeze until all juice is extracted. (Better wear plastic gloves that are disposable for this.)*

*Combine juice, sugar, and ginger ale. Pour into glasses. Add paraffin seals and lids. Store in refrigerator for 2 weeks.* Yield: 8 8-ounce glasses.

### Red Raspberry

*My favorite because of the tartness. Livens up biscuits, toast, or rolls. Also excellent filling for a jelly roll or for serving with fowl.*

2 quarts red raspberries
Sugar to measure

*Wash berries in strainer. Place in kettle and heat to boiling. Mash as they heat. Boil enough to obtain mush (about 5 minutes).*

*Pour mush into a strainer lined with damp cheesecloth (4 thicknesses). Allow juice to drip through for several hours.*

*Measure juice and boil for 10 minutes, uncovered. Add equal measure of sugar. Boil for another 5 minutes. Skim off scum. Use Chilled Plate Test (see Index) for thickness. (Skin should start to form on sample.)*

*Pour into glasses.* After *jelly has cooled and set (soft but firm), add paraffin seals and lids.* Yield: 6 5-ounce glasses.

### Grape

*This is a very easy recipe.*

2 cups bottled grape juice
3½ cups sugar
½ bottle fruit pectin

*Combine juice and sugar in a large saucepan. Mix well. Bring to a boil over high heat, stirring constantly. Stir in pectin immediately. Then bring to a full rolling boil for 1 minute, stirring constantly.*

*Remove from heat. Skim off foam with a metal spoon. Quickly pour into glasses. Add paraffin seals and lids.* Yield: 5 8-ounce glasses.

## Pineapple

1¾ cups canned unsweetened
  pineapple juice
¼ cup lemon juice

3½ cups sugar
½ bottle fruit pectin

*Combine juices and sugar in a large saucepan. Mix well. Bring to a boil over high heat, stirring constantly. Stir in pectin immediately. Then bring to a full rolling boil for 1 minute, stirring constantly.*

*Remove from heat. Skim off foam with a metal spoon. Quickly pour into glasses. Add paraffin seals and lids.* Yield: 5 8-ounce glasses.

## Wine

*This makes a good jelly.*

2 cups blackberry wine
3 cups sugar
½ bottle fruit pectin

*Mix wine and sugar in the top of a double boiler. Stir over rapidly boiling water until the sugar dissolves.*

*Remove from heat and immediately stir in pectin. Pour into glasses. Add paraffin seals and lids.* Yield: 5 8-ounce glasses.

## Fresh Mint

*An excellent gift for lamb fans. This is a fresh taste not available in the commercial jelly.*

1 cup coarsely chopped fresh
  mint
½ cup cider vinegar
1 cup water

3½ cups sugar
Green food coloring
¼ cup liquid pectin

*Wash mint and mash down slightly in a saucepan. Add vinegar, water, and sugar and bring to a boil. Add a few drops green food coloring. Bring to a boil and add pectin. Stir constantly. Bring to a rolling boil. Boil for ½ minute exactly.*

*Remove from heat. Skim. Strain into glasses. Add paraffin seals and lids.* Yield: 3 8-ounce glasses.

## Cranberry-Orange

*Very good flavor, as well as a pretty color.*

| | |
|---|---|
| 1½ cups orange juice | 1 package powdered fruit pectin |
| 2 cups bottled cranberry juice | 4 cups sugar |

*Mix juices and pectin and heat. Stir until it comes to a slow boil. Add sugar, bring to a rolling boil. Boil for 1 minute, stirring constantly.*

*Remove from heat. Skim off foam with a metal spoon. Pour into glasses. Add paraffin seals and lids. Yield: 7 6-ounce glasses.*

# BUTTERS

## English Lemon Butter

*A delicately flavored old favorite of English tea parties.*

| | |
|---|---|
| 6 eggs | 2 lemons (use grated rind and |
| 2 cups sugar | juice) |
| ¼ pound butter, melted | |

*Beat eggs until thoroughly mixed. Beat in sugar. Add butter. Cook in a double boiler until thick.*

*Add rind and juice. Cook until blended. Spoon into glasses. Add paraffin seals and lids. Yield: 3 8-ounce glasses.*

## Apple Butter

*A good old Pennsylvania Dutch treat. Popular everywhere, and always good for a quick snack spread.*

| | |
|---|---|
| 2 quarts pared, cored, sliced apples | ½ teaspoon cinnamon |
| ¾ pint boiling cider vinegar | ½ teaspoon cloves |
| ¾ pound brown sugar | ½ teaspoon allspice |

*Cut apples into bits, cover with water, and simmer until soft. Press through sieve. Add boiling cider vinegar. Stir in sugar. Cook until mixture begins to thicken. Add spices and stir until mixture becomes thick enough to spread at simmering heat.*

*Spoon into glasses. Add paraffin seals and lids. Yield: 6 8-ounce glasses.*

# MARMALADES

## Orange

*This English recipe is one of my husband's favorites on toast or muffins at breakfast or on biscuits for a late evening snack.*

| | |
|---|---|
| 1 dozen oranges | 2 quarts cold water |
| 4 lemons | 5 pounds sugar |

*Peel and cut the outer skins of the fruits into paper-thin strips. Soak peels in 2 quarts cold water for 24 hours.*

*The next day finely chop pulps and remove seeds. Tie seeds in a cheesecloth bag. Drop into pot while cooking fruit and water. Simmer chopped fruit and peel slowly for 2 hours.*

*Add sugar and cook until mixture jells. Use Chilled Plate Test (see Index) for desired thickness. Remove bag of seeds. Pour marmalade into glasses. Add paraffin seals and lids.* Yield: 8–10 8-ounce glasses.

## Apricot

*If you are a marmalade fan, this is a refreshingly new taste treat.*

| | |
|---|---|
| 1 pound dried apricots | 1 tablespoon grated lemon rind |
| 1½ cups sugar | 1 tablespoon grated orange rind |
| 6 tablespoons lemon juice | |

*Overnight, soak apricots, barely covered with cold water.*

*The next day, cook (covered) apricots until tender and puffy. Strain fruit and juice through a sieve.*

*Add the sugar, lemon juice, and rinds to 2 cups pulp. Cook, stirring constantly, over fairly high heat. (Mixture will become thick and waxy in about 15 minutes.)*

*Spoon into glasses. Add paraffin seals and lids.* Yield: 3 4-ounce glasses.

# Chapter 12

# THINGS TO MAKE

I am a make-it-yourselfer. When I was a child, Christmas, birthday, and anniversary cards complete with picture and verse were my specialties. Painting macaroni, hammering silver, tooling leather, and making craft items out of any and all spare parts I could lay my hands on filled the time between. As a teen-ager, I took to camp counseling, would you believe as an arts and crafts teacher?

To this day my attic is stuffed with scraps of this and that which my husband is forever hinting that I throw out. He simply cannot understand that in order to produce those unusual one-of-a-kind anniversary gifts or charming Christmas decorations you have to save from day to day and from season to season. If I need straw flowers for a Christmas centerpiece I can't pull them out of my sleeve on December 24. The attic beams hang with upside-down flowers drying? Okay, so duck when you go in there! You have to think ahead if you want people to gasp, "Oh, how clever!"

And where can you find milkweed pods in December or pine cones when the ground is covered with snow? Being a make-it-yourselfer has its hazards; piles of egg cartons, berry boxes, boxes of macaroni in all shapes marked, "Not for eating," bags of sewing scraps, empty cans in all sizes, popsicle sticks, and stacks and stacks of boxes. Is it worth it? Try it, but don't blame me if you get hooked!

Before we go into directions for making decorations and gifts for Christmas, let's take a minute to talk about gift wrapping. It is, of course, the first thing that you notice.

Christmas gifts should look gay, bright, and beautiful. Wrapping with love is so important. It shows that you cared. It also gives you a chance to be creative. Don't just wrap your packages in Christmas paper and tie a bow on top. Think about the person the gift is for and wrap with this in mind.

You can buy lovely papers, bows, and tie-ons for wrapping, but at best it is impersonal. Or you can use plain colored wrapping paper and draw pictures on it with colored marking pens, or cut tissue paper designs and paste them on for decoration. My daughter loves Charlie Brown characters and decorates her offerings with them. But non-artists can cut colored magazine illustrations or old Christmas card pictures to paste on their packages. You can co-ordinate the picture with the gift: a frozen pond scene for a gift of ice skates, a woman's face for a personal gift for a lady.

Or you can print your own gift paper!

## PRINTING GIFT PAPER

*This is lots of fun, but it can be messy. Make sure the working area is well covered with newspapers before you start.*

### Materials

Shelf paper in solid color, cut in desired lengths
Water-based paint of any color or colors
Very wide cereal bowl as paint container
Roller or rollers of different sizes (1″–3″)

### Method

*Dip and roll roller in paint. Move roller a few inches on the paper. Lift and move roller to a new area and repeat the process until done. Create design (crisscross, random, swirls, diamonds, checkerboard, overlays). Let paper and colors dry overnight before using.*

*Or cut a Bermuda onion in half. Dip half of the onion in paint. Press the onion onto the paper. Lift. It will leave an interesting circular design. Repeat process wherever you wish the design to appear on the paper.*

*A cabbage head cut in half will create another pattern for printing. Use the same printing process as with the onion. You can also use lemon slices, half a small onion, a wire whisk, or try using new materials to create your own personal creation.*

# WRAPPING GIFTS TO MAIL

*When it comes to mailing gifts, why let your Christmas packages arrive with crushed bows or mashed decorations? It is so easy to wrap them for traveling, yet give them that Christmas look. Of course, any gift looks great decorated as suggested below, even if you don't plan to mail it.*

## Materials

Christmas or plain wrapping
 paper
Boxes of colored stars in various
 sizes
Ribbons
Tempera paints

Glue
Sponge
Colored foil
Colored felt
Colored gummed paper
Self-stick tape

## Method

*After wrapping your package in either Christmas or plain paper:*

*Add a piece of colorful ribbon cut like an award ribbon with a star pasted below. Ink the star with the name of the gift recipient.*

*Cover the top of the box with stars of various sizes (in one color or many colors) in a random motif, or as in a constellation. Cut out a moon-shaped piece of gold foil to paste among the stars, with the name of the gift recipient written on it.*

*Dip sponge, cut to any size or shape you desire (Santa, tree, star), into thinned tempera paint. Touch it to the wrapping paper (plain white shelf paper) creating an all-over pattern. Finish the package with colored self-stick tape to complement the pattern.*

*Create designs with bands of self-stick tape in holiday patterns. (Especially good for tying up round packages.)*

*Cut Christmas trees, Christmas balls, snowflakes, candles, flowers, etc., from colored gummed paper and glue on in desired design.*

*Cut "NOEL" out of colored gummed paper and glue on. Or cut from colored felt or foil and glue on.*

*Glue lace doily onto paper (use doily of proper size for package). Glue a flat ribbon formed of holiday self-stick tape, or a design cut out of foil, in the center.*

Plate IV illustrates other suggestions for making your gift packaging more ingenious and amusing. Use these ideas to stimulate your own, and then go ahead and let your imagination have free reign.

By using foil, Christmas balls, ribbon, doilies, foam, braid, and even small trinkets from your five-and-dime store, you can create novel ideas to make your packages more exciting to make and to receive.

# TREE DECORATIONS

*Decorating the tree can become a creative project rather than one of taking the Christmas balls and tinsel down from the attic for yet another year. Why not use decorations from different countries to add new interest to your tree?*

## AUSTRIA

### Kripps

*These decorative diorama hangings are found on Austrian Christmas trees.*

*Use hollow polyethylene fruit. Cut an opening 1½" wide by 1¾" high in the side of the fruit, using a razor blade. Spray the interior with gold or silver paint. Dry. Frame the opening with 4 strips of self-adhering velvet ribbon. Glue gold or silver trimming to the ribbon. Cut small-scale scene from a Christmas card to approximately 2" wide and 2½" high. Stuff the back half of the fruit with crumpled tissue paper. Insert the picture into the opening in the fruit, curving it to form a diorama inside.*

## DENMARK

### Drums

*Colorful drums are popular on Danish trees.*

*Cut strips 10" long and 11½" wide from shirt cardboard. Staple to join ends. Cover open ends with white paper. Cover and glue sides with colored paper or self-adhering paper. Add strips of self-stick velvet strips around the edges to cover the joins. Use gold braid to trim, holding it in place with color-headed pins.*

# ENGLAND

## Cornucopia

*These hangings are traditional on English trees.*

*Paint cone-shaped paper cup diagonally with wide red stripes. Glue narrow strip of green ribbon around the top. Trim ribbon with tiny artificial flower cluster. Add ribbon handle for hanging.*

# FINLAND

## Himmeli

*Families get together to make these mobiles from straw at Christmas time in Finland. They use natural straw, but you can make them from drinking straws.*

**Materials:**

Straws
Long steel darning needle

Ball of heavy thread or tightly
   twisted string
Scissors

**Method:**

*Thread 4 straws and form into a square. Keep string taut. Thread 2 more straws at diagonal corners. Then 2 more at the other diagonal corners, forming a pyramid. Knot where possible for added strength. Now repeat process on underside and tie. String will be threaded through and back through straws, as necessary. Add a loop for hanging.*

# GERMANY

## Straw Stars

*Children have star-making parties in Germany before Christmas. They talk, sip spiced tea, and make straw stars for their trees.*

### Materials:

Wild oat and barley straw when turned golden
Rubber bands
Thread

### Method:

*Remove stem joints of the straw. Tie a handful with a rubber band and soak overnight in water that was brought to a boil. Weight down if necessary to keep underwater. The next day remove from water. Shake off excess water. Slit open lengthwise. Press flat and dry with a heavy iron.*

*To make the stars, arrange in multiples of 4. Form star by using pairs of strips with each pair forming a right angle cross. The top strip should fall to the right or left of the bottommost strip. To stitch together, weave thread from underneath star, bringing thread up and over the top strip, then immediately down under the bottom strip. Weave thread over and under the points of the star, binding together. Continue weaving until firmly anchored. Knot thread at the back of the star and make a hanging loop. Clip the ends of the straw to vary star shapes.*

# POLAND

## Porcupine

*Polish Christmas trees feature this decoration.*

*Cut, roll, and staple into cone shape strips of triangular paper. Brush touches of glue onto cones. Dust with sparkle. Staple, stitch, or tie together at broad end to form a pompon shape. Add ribbon for hanging.*

# RUSSIA

## Ornamental Christmas Balls

*This Russian ornament will really make your tree luxurious-looking.*

Cover round or teardrop-shaped Styrofoam ball with satin, velvet, or self-adhering paper in the pattern of your choice. Decorate further with braiding, sequins, artificial leaves or flowers pinned to the ball. Insert a 6″ length of pipe cleaner and curve the top end for a hanger.

# SWEDEN

## Tompte the Elf

*Tompte is always found on Swedish trees.*

Using a conical paper cup, paint the upper third (pointed end) red for a cap. Draw eyes, nose, and mouth into the middle third. Add cotton glued on for hair, eyebrows, mustache, and beard. Paint lower third blue for the body. Hook wire into the cap for hanging.

## UNITED STATES

### Plastic Spoon Ornaments

*Here's an American creation for the tree or good for decorating outdoors because it is weatherproof.*

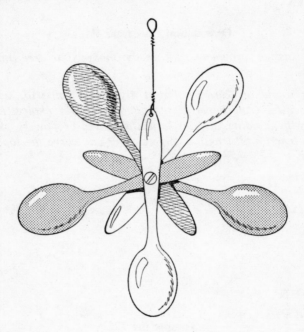

**Materials:**

Colored plastic spoons
Nuts and bolts
Hanging wire

**Method:**

*Arrange 5 spoons (same or different colors), all with bowls facing up, in a rosette. Drill a hole through the center where the spoons meet. Fasten together by using a nut and bolt. Drill another hole into the handle of one spoon for hanging wire to be attached.*

# GIFTS

### Tidbit Hanger

*Stack colorfully wrapped cheeses or cocktail tidbits in a wire lettuce washer. Tie a bow on the bottom. Tie the top ends together with ribbon for hanging. Top with a bow.*

### Soap Washcloth

*Sew 2 Christmas-printed washcloths together, leaving one end open to sew in a zipper. Fill with tiny pieces of fragrant-smelling soap to use as a soap pad in the bath. It can be refilled through the zippered end.*

### Photograph Christmas Ornament

*This makes a great gift to give to grandparents.*

**Materials:**

Profile photograph of head
India ink
Flashlight lenses (1½"–3",
  available in hardware stores)

Tape of colored fabric
Heavy thread

**Method:**

*Paint back of photograph with India ink. Cut head out carefully. Place photograph between lenses. Tape lenses together along edges. Loop heavy thread around rim. Leave a length free for hanging. To secure loop, use more tape.*

## Mitten Rack

*This is really a twofold gift. It delights the children, and it certainly makes life easier for the parents by keeping the house neater.*

**Materials:**

6 wooden clip clothespins
Enamel paint
Wooden bar (18″ long, 1″ wide, ½″ thick)

Self-adhering paper of desired pattern
6 large-headed upholstery nails
2 small screw eyes

**Method:**

*Paint clothespins, each a different color. Cover bar with self-adhering paper. Nail dry pins along edge of bar. Nail clips evenly distanced to the bar, putting the nail through one handle of the clip and having the top of the clip handle even with the top of the bar. Add screw eyes to top edge of the bar, 4″ from either end, for hanging.*

## Soap-Carving Set

*This makes a lovely creative gift for children and teen-agers too.*

**Materials:**

White floating soap
Smooth-edged paring knife or scout knife
Deep box

**Method:**

*Simply place the materials in the box and gift-wrap. The box will serve as a receptacle for the shavings of soap when the carver starts to work.*

## Styrofoam Storage

*This is great for keeping your children's crayons from breaking and getting scattered all over the place.*

**Materials:**

Block of Styrofoam
Sharp knife
Set of crayons

**Method:**

*Cut holes in the Styrofoam, evenly spaced, and round them with the knife. Place the crayons upright in the holes. The crayons can be seen for color selection, yet they are protected from breakage and neatly stored.*

## Car Container

*To keep your child amused on long car trips, and yet keep the car neat, try using this container.*

**Materials:**

Metal cake pan with sliding cover
Paint

**Method:**

*Paint child's name and perhaps some picture or design on the lid. Fill with coloring book, crayons, or whatever paraphernalia amuses your child.*

## Shoe Bag Surprise Package

*Great fun for car travel or the sickroom. This will keep the children busy and out of your hair.*

**Materials:**

Colorful material shoe bag with pockets
Crayons and paper
Magnetic checkers

Clay and molds
Paper dolls and blunt scissors
Cat's-cradle string

**Method:**

*Place these items, or any others you know will interest your child, in the shoe bag pockets. But, on the outside of these pockets pin the following signs:*

1   *Don't open until you have counted 21 cows.*
2   *Don't open until you find a license plate number with 327 in it.*
3   *Play ticktacktoe; the winner may open this pocket.*
4   *See how many words you can make out of name of destination.*
5   *Print the words LET'S HAVE FUN. Players must check off each letter from passing signs before they open this pocket.*

## Rollaway Toy Chest

*An easy way to create a space-saver that's fun.*

**Materials:**

An inexpensive bookcase or an old one you may have
Casters

**Method:**

*Place bookcase on its back and put on casters underneath at all four corners. (You may paint or cover the bookcase with self-adhering paper if you wish to dress it up.) The case will now be able to be rolled under the child's bed as a rollaway toy chest, complete with compartments.*

## Window Gift Box

*This makes a pretty gift that you can fill with whatever pleases you.*

**Materials:**

Shoe box or hatbox
Self-adhering paper of desired
    design

Plastic wrap
Cellophane tape

**Method:**

*Cut a window in the bottom small end of the box. Leave ½″ margin of the box around the window. Cover the window with a piece of plastic wrap cut to size. Tape securely on all 4 sides to the box. Cover the outside, top, and bottom of the box (except for the window) with self-adhering paper.*

## Cookie Bucket Gift Box

*An easy way to obtain an attractive cookie container.*

**Materials:**

1 oatmeal box (the round kind)
Self-adhering paper of desired design

**Method:**

*Cover outside of the box and the lid top with the paper. Add a sprig of holly to the top for extra decoration.*

### Flip-Lid Gift Box

*Great gift box for men's hankies, socks, etc.*

**Materials:**

1 cigar box
Self-adhering paper of desired design

**Method:**

*Cover the box and line it with the paper. Add a sprig of evergreen, with small Christmas balls tied on, to the top of the box for decoration.*

# DECORATIONS FOR THE HOUSE

## Sunbursts

*These decorations are good on a large Christmas tree indoors or out.*

**Materials:**

| | |
|---|---|
| Clean, dry, lidless cans of various sizes | Household cement |
| Tin snippers | Glitter |

**Method:**

*Cut each can down the sides to the base at regular intervals around the cylinder.* Be careful of sharp edges.

*Bend the strips down to create a basic sunflower form. Use your ingenuity in clipping the petal edges or rolling or twisting them to create different forms. Glitter or other ornaments can be added for a desired effect with household cement.*

*Very large cans can have their petals ornamented with smaller cans cut in varied shapes and cemented on.*

## Hanging Christmas Banner

*These are very effective on doors, walls, or windows.*

**Materials:**

Cut-out colored felt forms (Santa, etc.) or designs or lettering (Noel)

Felt or fabric banner (6' long by 19" wide)

Bells

Ribbons

Colored drapery rope

Colored fringe

**Method:**

*Glue designs to the banner for the desired effect. Sew on bells, ribbons, etc., where desired. Stitch rope to top of banner for hanging. Sew fringe to bottom of banner for a finished look.*

## Pine Cone Wreath

*This is an easy way to create one of those lovely cone wreaths that cost so much to buy in the stores.*

**Materials:**

Spool of wire

Pine cones of varying sizes

Florist's picks

1 Styrofoam wreath

Wire clippers

**Method:**

*Wire the large cones singly to a pick. Wire the smaller cones in a group to one pick. Poke sticks into the foam, covering the entire wreath, to create a fully decorated wreath of cones.*

## Christmas Ball Wreath

*This makes a gaily colored wreath lighting up your door or mantel.*

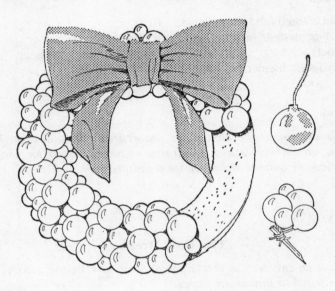

### Materials:

Pipe cleaners
Airplane glue
Miniature Christmas balls
Spool of wire

Florist's picks
1 Styrofoam wreath
Wire clippers

### Method:

Dip the ends of the pipe cleaners into glue, then insert them into the necks of the Christmas balls. Wire the balls in clusters to the florist's picks. Poke the picks into the foam wreath to create a fully decorated wreath of Christmas balls.

## Decorated Yule Log

*The traditional foundation for the Christmas Eve fire can be decorated and burned and consumed entirely.*

**Materials:**

Paraffin
Oak log, fireplace size, split
    lengthwise to give it a flat
    surface to rest on

Evergreen boughs
Cones
Holly
Berries

**Method:**

*Melt the paraffin in the top of a double boiler. Cool it for about 30 minutes until you can touch and mold it. Pile some paraffin on the top center of the log. Press the evergreen boughs into it, making a fan-like arrangement. Arrange cones, holly, and berries in center. This makes a nice gift, or it can be used to decorate your own fireplace.*

## Kissing Ring

*This too can be used in your own home or as a gift.*

**Materials:**

2 embroidery hoops
Ribbon
Wire

Mistletoe
Small bells
Bow

**Method:**

*Cover the hoops with ribbon. Insert one hoop at right angles inside the other, forming a cross. Wire together at the top and bottom meeting points. Wire mistletoe to the top point. Hang bells from the bottom point with ribbon. Place the bow on top and make a ribbon loop for hanging.*

## Wall Wreath Tree

*Something a little different.*

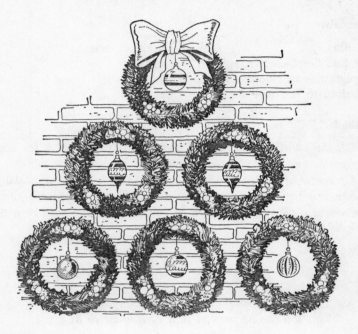

**Materials:**

6 wreaths                                    6 Christmas balls
Heavy-duty nylon fish cord                   Velvet ribbon bow

**Method:**

Hang the wreaths on the wall in a pyramid-tree form with the cord.
Center and hang a Christmas ball in each wreath. Top the tree form
with the bow.

Plate IV.   Some new ideas on Christmas gift wrapping.
*CPS Industries, Inc., CPS Plaza, Pittsburgh, Pa. 15238.*

## Pine Cone Flowers

*These make pretty, and durable, decorations.*

**Materials:**

Pine cones of varying sizes          Wire
Paints                               Green crepe paper

**Method:**

Cut top of each cone away. Paint remaining part of cone to create a petal effect, while painting the center another color to make the cone look like a flower (zinnia). Hook wire around the base of the cone to make a stem. Cover wire with green crepe paper for a realistic effect.

## Glowing Flowers

**Materials:**

5 pieces (3" by 4" rectangles) colored tissue paper
Florist's wire
Florentine wax

**Method:**

*Stack papers. Tie them together at the center with florist's wire. Pull the paper forward with moistened fingers, arranging in a rosette. Roll the edges of each petal.*

*Melt 2" of wax in a pan. Dip the flower. Shake off excess wax. The flower will dry in seconds.*


## Yarn Daisies

*These make a very colorful bouquet.*

**Materials:**

1 7-ounce skein heavy rug yarn
    (makes 18 4" daisies or 13 5"
    daisies)
Stiff cardboard (4½" wide for
    small flowers, 5½" for large)

Glue
Sequins
Green thread

**Method:**

*Wind yarn around cardboard, one loop next to the other (18 times for the large flower, 14 times for smaller ones). Slip loops off carefully and place across a 3" length of yarn. Tie loops tightly in center. Cut off ends at center. Pull each loop to the side to look like daisy petals. Glue a sequin in the center. Attach to the tree as a hanging decoration, by using green thread drawn through a few loops. Or you can sew, spaced at intervals, along a long ribbon to make a table decoration. Or you can wire the flowers with stems and stick them into Styrofoam to use as a centerpiece.*

## Pompon Hangings

*Lovely on tree, window, or mantel.*

### Materials:

Wool yarns of various colors
Postcard-size piece of cardboard
Cardboard piece a bit smaller
   than postcard size

Cardboard piece still smaller than
   those above

### Method:

*Wind brightly colored wool yarn around postcard-size card. Slip a length of yarn through the top of the loops and tie in a knot. Remove tied yarn. Cut loop ends so that a thick pompon forms.*

*Make another pompon on the second card in another shade or color of yarn. Then make a third pompon still smaller on the smallest card.*

*Tie the 3 pompons together in a line. Add a loop of yarn for hanging to the top pompon.*

## Macaroni Decorations

*Good for hanging on trees, in windows, from the mantel.*

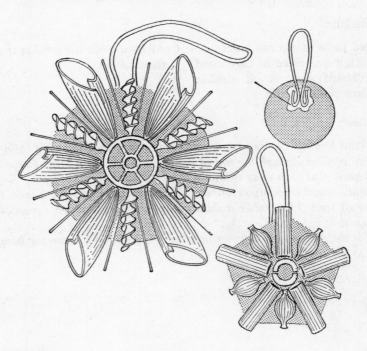

### Materials:

Colored cardboard disks 2″–3″ in diameter
Differently shaped macaroni
Transparent glue

### Method:

Create design (*snowflake, rosette, wreath, medallion*) by gluing macaroni onto each disk. Glue a yarn loop to the back for hanging.

## Hanging Berry Flower Container

**Materials:**

Plastic berry container
Colorful ribbon
Styrofoam square to fit bottom
of container

Artificial poinsettias or other
desired flowers or greens
Clay

**Method:**

*Lace container with ribbon. Place foam in bottom. Poke flower stems into foam. Anchor with a bit of clay stuck around as needed.*

## Mailbox Decorations

*Be sure to use weatherproof materials. Keep it simple. Use plastic ribbon and evergreen boughs.*

## Apartment House Door Decoration

*Use a brightly arranged wreath with a red cellophane bow to add gleam to the wreath and spray snow for a lightening effect in a dark hallway. Add bells so a welcome will ring when the door is opened.*

## Umbrella Stand Decoration

*It is best to keep this simple. A pine bough and bow should suffice.*

## Screen Card Display

*An attractive way to display your Christmas cards is to pin them to a three-fold screen covered with green and red felt panels.*

# FOR A PARTY

## Balloon Invitation

*Something novel in the way of sending a party invitation is to blow up a balloon and write the message of the invitation on it with a felt-tipped pen. Then deflate and slip into an envelope as an invitation and preparty favor.*

### Edible Place Cards

*Bake cookies and ice them with the names of your guests. Prop cookies in place at the table by using toothpicks.*

# CHRISTMAS-DECORATED TABLECLOTHS

### Felt Runner

*May be used on table or mantel.*

*Scallop the edges of a length of colored felt that has been cut to table or mantel size. Glue grosgrain ribbon down the center of the strip lengthwise. Decorate the ribbon by stitching at intervals rosettes of multicolored felt, or yarn pompons, or fancy-tied bows. Or you can glue pine cones or Christmas balls in the designs of your choosing.*

### Designed Felt Cloth

**Materials:**

Glue
Sequins
Green felt cut-out trees of varying sizes

White felt cut-out stars of varying sizes
Red felt tablecloth

**Method:**

*Glue sequins onto the trees for sparkle. Then glue the cutouts around the border of the cloth.*

### Christmas Package Table

**Materials:**

Broad red ribbon
White tablecloth

Large bow
Pine sprays

**Method:**

*Lay ribbon on tablecloth to form a cross in the center. Anchor with occasional stitches. Top the center with a large bow. Tuck the pine sprays around the bow, extending them somewhat down the ribbon lengths on all 4 sides. (Optional: Place Christmas balls around the sprays for color.)*

## CHRISTMAS DECORATIONS AND CENTERPIECES

### Birch Log Centerpiece

**Materials:**

Drill
Birch log cut to table size
Candles

Evergreens
Holly

**Method:**

*In the log drill holes sized for your candles. Place candles. Set log on a bed of evergreens decorated with holly (real or artificial).*

### Nut Tree Centerpiece

**Materials:**

12″ Styrofoam cone
Glue
4–5 pounds assorted nuts
(walnuts, filberts, Brazil,
almonds, pecans, pistachios)

Gold-painted walnut
Green food coloring
Gold foil leaves

**Method:**

*Work around cone gluing a ring of assorted nuts around the base of the tree. Allow to dry thoroughly. Glue on other rings the same way until the cone is completely covered. Top with a gold-painted walnut. Color some pistachios green with food coloring. Dry thoroughly before gluing into any spaces between the nuts. Add gold foil leaves in the spaces with the green pistachios.*

## Tin Can Christmas Tree

*Makes an unusual centerpiece.*

**Materials:**

33 same-sized cans with tops and
   bottoms out
Spray paint in one color or
   desired colors

1 spray paint can in black
Dark green pipe cleaners

**Method:**

*Punch 4 equidistant holes around each can top and bottom. Spray can interiors with desired colors. Spray can exteriors black. Dry. Wire cans together into a pyramid tree form with the pipe cleaners. Use 3 cans with 2 cans on top for the tree trunk.*

## Christmas Ball Tree

*This makes a very colorful centerpiece.*

**Materials:**

Glue
38 3″ Christmas balls
1 Styrofoam disk
5 Styrofoam rings (2″, 4″, 6″,
   8″, 10″)

2 small-bead garlands
   (separated)
2 large-bead garlands
   (separated)
Box large-headed straight pins
Evergreens

**Method:**

*Place and glue 12 balls near the edge around the disk (ring end pointing inward). Dry. Glue 10 balls onto the 10-inch ring; 7 on the 8-inch ring; 5 on the 6-inch ring; 3 on the 4-inch ring; dry. Stack and glue in position as you form tree shape. Glue 2-inch ring to the top and glue a Christmas ball in the center. Dry.*

*Pin beads around the edges of the disk and rings with small and large beads alternating. Poke in greens along disk between the Christmas balls.*

## Curly Tin Can Christmas Tree

*This makes an unusual centerpiece and will create a real conversation piece.*

**Materials:**

1 can with top and bottom lids off
Heavy scissors
Small gumdrops

**Method:**

*Hold can horizontally. Place in wall-type can opener and cut off rim completely. Now place can in opener in a horizontal position and cut, starting at the seam and going around up to but not including the seam. The rim of the can will remain attached to the seam. It will be the tree base. The seam will be the tree trunk.*

*Now cut the can down the center, opposite the seam. Flatten the can out. Cut the can sides in narrow strips to the seam but not through it. Strips will curl when cut. Adjust the curls to form a uniform tree. Pull some curls up for cone shape. Trim the ends with gumdrops.*

## Mesh Tree Centerpiece

*Another interesting decoration for the table or mantel.*

**Materials:**

Length of mesh to desired tree size
Sphagnum moss
Evergreen twigs
Cellophane-wrapped lollipops
Artificial holly berries wired in bunches
Round red tray or large plate

**Method:**

*Roll mesh to cone form. Wire closed. Fill inside of cone with wet moss. Poke evergreens into mesh to cover and fill out tree. Add lollipops and berries poked into the wire between the greens. Set on tray or plate.*

## Driftwood Tree Centerpiece

**Materials:**

Driftwood branch
White spray paint
Small red Christmas balls

**Method:**

*Spray branch with paint. Dry. Tie balls onto branches. This is very effectively used on a dark green cloth with white candles in holders set on either end.*

## Yarn Christmas Tree Centerpiece

**Materials:**

Styrofoam tree form
Glue
Yarn or yarns of desired colors

Small bells, Christmas balls, miniature toys

**Method:**

*Paint foam tree with glue. Wind yarn around entire tree, one thread immediately next to the other. Then stitch on decorations to suit your taste.*

## Table Crèche

**Materials:**

Crèche figures, barn, animals
Styrofoam disk

3 white candles of varying sizes
Greens

**Method:**

*Arrange scene on disk. Place candles into foam in the background of the scene. Poke greens into foam edge, shorter greens in the front, taller ones in the rear.*

## Madonna Table Top

**Materials:**

Ceramic or wooden madonna
Tall white candle
Styrofoam disk

2 lily-of-the-valley sprays with
 white net bow at the base
Greens

**Method:**

*Place madonna on disk. Slightly to her left rear place the candle
into the foam. Arrange one lily-of-the-valley spray at the base of
the madonna and spread it toward the candle. Poke greens in low
arrangement around the edge of the foam. Tie the second spray of
lilies in among front greenery.*

## Madonna Driftwood Table Top

**Materials:**

Ceramic madonna
Flat oblong piece of driftwood

Spray of white statice
Gray clay

**Method:**

*Place madonna on wood to right front. Arrange statice in a spray
behind her to the left rear by sticking the stems into a blob of clay
placed on the wood.*

## Madonna and Child Mantel Scene

**Materials:**

3 lengths of wood graduated in
 length
Madonna and Child statue

Pine branches
6 votive candles

**Method:**

*Place longest wood length on the mantel. Top with the next
length, then shortest length. Arrange tall branch behind the top
length. Tuck greenery in and surround the front wood lengths. Place
3 candles on 1 side, in step-like arrangement, 1 on each level. Do*

*the same on the other side. Place statue on top length of wood in front of pine branches.*

## Christmas Eve Carolers

**Materials:**

Snow-sprayed miniature artificial tree with tiny Christmas balls
Circular wrought-iron candle-holder
Candles
Ceramic caroler figurines
Spray snow

**Method:**

*Place tree in center opening of candleholder. Put candles in holder. Place figurines outside and surrounding the candleholder. Spray snow on scene.*

## Santa Centerpiece

**Materials:**

Spray snow
8 artificial miniature trees in varying sizes
3 cardboard houses
1 6″ Styrofoam disk
1 miniature Santa in sleigh with reindeer

**Method:**

*Spray snow on trees and house roofs. Set up houses and some trees on the disk. Place Santa in sleigh with reindeer on the disk. Group the rest of the trees in a semicircle around the scene. Spray scene lightly with snow.*

## Choir Boy Centerpiece

**Materials:**

3 choir boy molded candles
1 Styrofoam disk
1 lamppost molded candle
Evergreen twigs

**Method:**

*Stand choir boys on foam under lamppost. Nail figures from underside of foam to secure. Poke twigs into the edge of the disk to create a greenery effect. Use short twigs in front of the boys, taller ones to the rear as a backdrop.*

## Muffin Tin Centerpiece

**Materials:**

Red spray paint
1 muffin tin
12 votive candles

Evergreen boughs
Small Christmas balls

**Method:**

*Spray muffin tin. Set in candles. Arrange boughs around muffin tin. Tie Christmas balls to boughs in random arrangement.*

## Cardboard Candle Centerpiece

**Materials:**

Cardboard tubes from foil or plastic wrap
Self-adhering paper in design of choice

Gold tissue paper
Styrofoam ring
Evergreen clippings

**Method:**

*Cover tubes with self-adhering paper. Stuff a piece of tissue paper in the top to represent the flame of a candle. Cut circles in the foam ring for the tubes. Place tubes into foam ring. Poke greens into and around the ring to cover.*

## Oleo Container Centerpiece

**Materials:**

Round oleomargarine container, the brand with exterior gold finish
Green clay
Artificial pine and holly clusters

**Method:**

*Pack container with clay. Poke evergreen clusters into the clay in desired arrangement.*

## Star Candles for the Table

**Materials:**

Star-shaped ashtray
Foil
Colored granulated candle wax and wick

**Method:**

*Cover ashtray with foil. Fill star with wax and insert wick.*

## Fishbowl Centerpiece

**Materials:**

Candle                                    Melted wax or clay
Round fishbowl with wide top    Evergreen twigs
   opening                                 Christmas balls of varying sizes

**Method:**

*Fasten candle to bottom of bowl with melted wax or clay. Arrange greens around the base of the candle. Place balls on greens for desired effect.*

## Making a "12 Days of Christmas" Candle

*This is a nice custom. You can burn the candle to the mark on each day of the Twelve Days of Christmas.*

**Materials:**

1 teaspoon salt
2 teaspoons borax
⅓ cup water
1 yard soft white string
A little melted candle wax
Small piece of cardboard
Masking tape
1¼ pounds paraffin
1¼ pounds beeswax
Colored wax crayons

1-quart mold (milk carton with ends off for a square candle; mailing tube for a round candle)
Small block of ice
Colored magic marker
Optional: sequins, glitter, metallic tape, braid, charms, etc.

**Method:**

*Paraffin drips freely because of a low melting point. Beeswax hardens the candle. For an all-beeswax candle use 2½ pounds beeswax.*

### Wick Directions

*Make a day or so in advance of the candle.*

*Dissolve salt and borax in water. Soak string in it for 2 hours. Remove the string and dry. This solution keeps the wick from fizzing out or burning too rapidly.*

*Cut string 2 inches or more longer than needed for wick length of mold. Melt a small amount of wax in the top of a double boiler and dip the wick in. Remove the wick and allow wax to drip down, then dip again. Hang wick straight to dry. Wick is ready to use when wax has stiffened the string and it is completely dry.*

### Candle Directions

*Before pouring wax place wick. Cut a square or circle of cardboard to cover the end of the mold you are using. Punch a hole in the center of it. Make a knot in one end of the wick, pull wick through the hole. Knot will anchor it. Tape cardboard to one end of the tube, wick hanging down inside.*

*Melt paraffin and beeswax in the top of a double boiler. Don't let them get smoking hot. Color by shaving colored wax crayons into the melted wax. One crayon will color this amount. For darker shades use 2 crayons, 3 for white or black. For pastels use ¼ to ½ a crayon. Stir well to blend.*

*Stand mold on a piece of ice when pouring hot wax in so that it hardens immediately and will not run out. Pull wick straight through the tube and hold steady in the center as the wax is poured. After the wax hardens, peel tube off. Rub the candle with a soft cloth rubbed with wax to polish it gently.*

## Decorations

*Use a colored magic marker to mark off 12 lines and write numbers for the Twelve Days of Christmas. Or you can draw designs on the candle and decorate it with sequins, glitter, metallic tape or braid, ornaments, charms, small bells, artificial flowers, leaves, colored stars, etc.*

*In sprinkling glitter, redip finished candle into a bath of melted wax of the same color. Drain briefly; do not allow to harden. Sprinkle with glitter. Dry.*

*Other decorations are stuck to the candle with drops of melted wax of the same color, or stuck by short straight pins directly into the candle.*

*To write Noel or Merry Christmas on the candle, use gold or silver letters that come in paper sheets to push out. Stick the letters to the candle with melted wax.*

# Chapter 13

# THINGS ESPECIALLY FOR CHILDREN TO MAKE

Children love to make things for family giving. Here are some ideas, some simple, others a little more complex, but all easy enough to be completed without an adult doing most of it. Some items are so easy that a young child can manage with a minimum of supervision.

## GIFTS FOR OTHER CHILDREN

### One-of-a-Kind Place Mats

**Materials:**

A child's drawing signed by the creator (message can be included)
Adhesive-backed clear plastic

**Method:**

*Cover both sides of the drawing with plastic to make a colorful and personal gift that is washable.*

### Christmas Napkin Ring

*This can be co-ordinated with the place mat.*

**Materials:**

Snap, needle, thread
Red felt cut with pinking shears
 (1½" by 7" strips)

Fabric glue
Small green felt Christmas trees
Sequins

**Method:**

*Sew a snap to each strip so it will fasten to form a ring. Have ends overlap 1".*

*Glue trees to the top of each ring (as many as desired). Glue sequins to the trees to decorate them.*

### Santa Place Card

*This can be used at the party table or can be tied to gifts.*

**Materials:**

| | |
|---|---|
| Glue | 2 black felt eyes |
| Cotton | 1 red felt nose |
| Cone-shaped paper cup | 1 red felt mouth |

**Method:**

*Glue cotton to the top of the cup and around the front edge to form a beard. Glue on felt eyes, nose, mouth, and cotton eyebrows and mustache. Write name of person across forehead.*

### Marshmallow Snowman

*Can be used as a table decoration for a party or as a party favor.*

**Materials:**

| | |
|---|---|
| 3 marshmallows for each man | 1 small cookie per man |
| Paste of confectioners' sugar and | 1 large cookie per man |
|    a little milk with vegetable | 1 cherry per man |
|    coloring added | 2 toothpicks per man |

**Method:**

*Stick snowman together by using paste between the marshmallows to make the body. Use colored paste for the eyes, nose, and mouth. Use small cookie for a hat and put it on with paste. Top hat with a cherry. Place man on a large cookie and anchor him with paste. Add toothpick arms.*

## Apple-Face Santa

**Materials:**

Paste

Cotton

Cone-shaped red paper cup

1 apple

2 raisins

Toothpicks

1 cherry

**Method:**

*Paste cotton around the edge of the cup and at the top point for decoration. Use cup as a hat for Santa. Place a small piece of cotton on the apple for eyebrows. Pull a small piece of that cotton down to anchor same by placing raisins over the piece and sticking them into the apple with toothpicks to make eyes. Add a cherry for a nose, anchor with a toothpick. Drape cotton around the bottom of the apple for a beard. Anchor with bits of toothpick under the hat.*

## Gumdrop Candlestick

**Materials:**

1 tiny candle

1 large gumdrop

1 colored lifesaver

**Method:**

*Place candle in the middle of the gumdrop. Fit lifesaver into side of gumdrop to create a handle for the candlestick.*

## Tree Lapel Pin

**Materials:**

Green felt

Pinking shears

Small safety pin, needle, thread

Fabric cement

Sequins

**Method:**

*Cut felt into tree form with the pinking shears. Sew the pin to the back of the tree. Cement sequins to the tree for decoration.*

## Photo Puzzle

**Materials:**

Paste                                    Cardboard
Photo of desired subject                 Scissors

**Method:**

*Paste photo to cardboard. Cut into irregular shapes, so that when the puzzle is put together again it will become the original picture.*

## Personalized Trash Can

**Materials:**

Decals
Plastic or metal trash can (plain)
Paint

**Method:**

*Add decal to desired spot on can. Paint name or message above or below it to personalize it.*

## Personalized Switch Plate

**Materials:**

Paint
Blank switch plate

**Method:**

*Paint name at the top of the plate. Draw a picture or design across the bottom.*

### Child's Room Mailbox

**Materials:**

1 napkin box with top cut off as stated in box directions
Self-adhering paper of desired design
Bells, bow, sprig of holly

**Method:**

*Cover outside of box with paper. Poke a hole in the top rear of the box for hanging. Decorate further as desired by adding bells, bow, small sprig of holly.*

### Powder Puff Santa

**Materials:**

Glue
Colored paper cut for
  eyes, nose, and mouth

Powder puff
Triangular piece of foil for cap
Cotton

**Method:**

*Glue paper features to puff to create a face. Add cap. Glue cotton to face to make a beard, eyebrows, and hair.*

### Gift Tubes

**Materials:**

Toilet paper or toweling tubes
Candies and miniature toys

Christmas paper or self-adhering
  paper
Ribbon

**Method:**

*Fill tubes with candies and miniature toys. Then either wrap the tubes in lengths of Christmas paper, tying the ends with bright ribbon, or cover tube with self-adhering paper, then fill.*

# GIFTS AND DECORATIONS FOR ADULTS

*Making something for Dad, or Grandma, or Aunt Paula is something many children look forward to at Christmas time. These are some ideas they can handle easily.*

## Paperweight Stones

**Materials:**

Glue
Poster paints
Washed stones

**Method:**

*By adding a few drops of glue to your paints smooth brushing will be easy.*
*Paint designs, flowers, or pictures on the stones in bright colors.*

## Animal Rocks

**Materials:**

Stones of unusual shapes          Glue
Magic marker                      Felt, cotton, net, etc.

**Method:**

*Wash stones and dry thoroughly. Design each into an animal by making features with a magic marker and gluing on felt, cotton, net, etc., to create the animal (e.g., rabbit—cotton tail and nose, felt ears).*

## Sweet Sewing

**Materials:**

Sweet-smelling soap
Needles threaded with different colors

**Method:**

*Stud soap with needles so when ready to sew needles slide easily and make material smell good.*

## Clamshell Soap Dish

**Materials:**

| | |
|---|---|
| Clamshell | Sequins |
| Gold or silver spray paint | Small fancy soaps |
| Glue | Plastic wrap |

**Method:**

*Spray clamshell with paint. Dry. Glue sequins to the hinge. Place small soaps on shell. Cover with plastic wrap.*

## Winter Herb Garden

**Materials:**

| | |
|---|---|
| Washed and dried cans with lids off | Dirt |
| Self-adhering paper of desired pattern | Parsley and chive seeds |

**Method:**

*Cover cans with paper. Fill with dirt. Plant seeds as directed on seed packages.*

## Pop Art Bottles

**Materials:**

| | |
|---|---|
| Soda or wine bottles | Paints of desired colors |
| White paint | Brushes |

**Method:**

*Give bottles a white undercoating. Then paint on designs or pic-*

*tures in the colors you wish. Let your imagination swing . . . make
them way out!*

### Picture Flip Calendar

## Materials:

Hole punch
Colored construction paper (you
can use a different color for
each month)
Glue

Colored magazine picture or
postcards appropriate to
each month
1 small calendar, with each
month on a different sheet
Colored yarn

**Method:**

*Punch 2 holes along length edge of paper. Glue a picture to the top half of each page (one for each month). Glue the appropriate month below each picture.*

*Thread yarn through holes and tie in a bow. As each month passes, it can be flipped over to reveal a new month and picture.*

*(If this is a gift for grandparents, have your child draw a picture for each month. Or if you are very ambitious, make each picture an appropriate photograph of the children, family, house, or pets.)*

### Recipe Book

**Materials:**

Loose-leaf notebook

Self-adhering paper of choice

Indexed dividers and labels

Blank pages for notebook

Paste

Table of weights and measures

**Method:**

*Cover the loose-leaf book with the paper. Add the indexed dividers and label (bread, vegetables, etc., as in a cookbook). Place blank pages between indexed areas to be used for recipes. Paste table of weights and measures to the inside of the front cover. It comes in handy!*

### Sewing or Knitting Box

*This makes a lovely gift for Grandma or Auntie or Mother.*

**Materials:**

Hatbox

Self-adhering paper in desired pattern

Threads, needles, pin cushion,

scissors, pins, tape measure; or knitting needles, yarn, tape measure

**Method:**

*Cover the outside of the hatbox and the lid top with the paper. Fill the box with either the sewing kit or knitting kit.*

## Christmas Matchboxes

**Materials:**

Boxes of matches
Self-adhering paper in desired pattern

**Method:**

*Cover outside of the boxes with paper, for a colorful and easy-to-make gift that comes in handy.*

## Jewelry Carton

**Materials:**

Gold spray paint
Egg cartons with individual cups

**Method:**

*Spray cartons. Dry. These make good storage bins for keeping jewelry sorted and easily visible. The spray paint disguises their origin, and they look nice in a drawer.*

## Pencil Holder

**Materials:**

1 can with lid off
Self-adhering paper in desired design

**Method:**

*Cover outside of the can with paper. Add a sprig of holly and a bow to decorate it further if you wish.*

## Artistic Plant Container

**Materials:**

Flowerpot
Self-adhering paper in desired design

Glue
Colored yarn

## Method:

*Cover pot with paper. Ring top outside rim of pot with glue. Wind a few rows of yarn (one or many colors) around the top rim and press into the glue. Dry.*

*or*

*Paint the outside of the pot with glue, then wrap rows of the colored yarn around the entire outside of the pot. Press into the glue.*

*or*

*Place the pot in a white paint bucket (from hardware or paint store) and decorate the bucket with paper or foil cutouts or with stripes of colored holiday tape.*

### Gold Mesh Gift Bag

## Materials:

| | |
|---|---|
| Mesh orange or onion bag | Bells |
| Gold spray paint | Greens |
| Bows | Pine cones |

## Method:

*Spray bag with paint. Dry thoroughly. (This makes a lovely gift when filled with foodstuffs, candy, or small toys.) Decorate with bows, bells, greens, pine cones, as desired.*

### Powder Puff Angel

## Materials:

| | |
|---|---|
| Powder puff | Glue |
| Crayons | Pipe cleaner (yellow) |
| Foil | |

## Method:

*Draw a face on the puff with the crayons. Cut wings from the foil and glue them to the back of the puff. Cut foil fringe for hair and glue to forehead. Bend pipe cleaner into a halo shape and glue to the back of the head.*

*If you should want to hang this from your tree, add a loop of yarn for hanging.*

## GIFTS FOR PETS

### Christmas Box Home for a Cat

**Materials:**

Cardboard box from the grocer
Self-adhering paper in desired pattern, Christmas-looking
Colorful pillow

**Method:**

*Cover the box with the paper. Add the pillow to make the inside more comfortable for your pet. (Size box and pillow to the size of your pet.)*

### Dog Toy

**Materials:**

A small Christmas stocking
Rags

**Method:**

*Stuff stocking foot with the rags. Tie a firm knot or two where rags end. Your dog will love to pull on the stuffed end while you hang onto the leg end of the stocking.*

## DECORATIONS FOR THE TREE

### Name Christmas Balls

**Materials:**

Plain Christmas balls
Glue
Glitter

**Method:**

*Spell out name on balls with glue. Add glitter to glued part of the balls. Name will then be spelled out in glitter.*

## Porcupine Balls

**Materials:**

Colored Christmas beads          Styrofoam Christmas balls
Chenille pipe cleaners           Wire

**Method:**

*Thread beads on pipe cleaners cut in varying lengths. Insert cleaner ends into each ball to create an over-all porcupine effect. Run a wire with a hooked end through from top to bottom for hanging.*

## Sequin Balls

**Materials:**

Small straight pins              Foam Christmas balls
Sequins                          Wire

**Method:**

*Stick pins through sequins and pin sequins all over each ball for a glittering effect. Run a wire with a hooked end through from top to bottom of the ball for hanging.*

## Foil Tree Ornaments

**Materials:**

8½″ by 11″ piece of foil         Cellophane tape
Colored construction paper       Loop for hanging

**Method:**

*Fold piece of foil in half lengthwise. Double again but don't fold. Cut designs into the foil from both edges. Unfold and center foil on a piece of colored construction paper of same size. Pick up both papers together and roll into a cylinder. Tape the edges to hold. Attach loop for hanging.*

## Silver-Ring Ornaments

**Materials:**

1" rings cut from cardboard foil    1" Christmas  balls
   tubes                        Heavy thread
Foil                             Bright  bows

**Method:**

*Cover rings with foil. Hang the balls inside the rings and tie to the top with thread. Add the bows on top of the rings to decorate (one ball and bow per ring).*

## Bead-Ring Ornaments

**Materials:**

1" rings cut from cardboard foil   Wire
   tube                        Beads
Foil

**Method:**

*Cover rings with foil. Wire beads entirely around each ring.*

## Foreign Doll Ornaments

**Materials:**

Small plastic foreign dolls
Colored yarn

**Method:**

*Tie dolls to Christmas tree branches with yarn.*

## Rock Candy Ornaments

**Materials:**

String
Rock candy

**Method:**

*Add some string to the existing string that is already on the candy. Tie to branches of the Christmas tree to give the appearance of frosty crystals of ice hanging.*

## Gumdrop Ornaments

**Materials:**

Colored gumdrops
Narrow rickrack

**Method:**

*Thread gumdrops with the rickrack and tie to Christmas tree branches.*

## Chocolate Kiss Ornaments

**Materials:**

Chocolate kisses in silver paper
Colored thread

**Method:**

*Tie kisses with thread and hang from branches of the Christmas tree.*

## Christmas Plaques

**Materials:**

Rubber cement or clay          Bits of greens
Ribbon                         Paper angels, Santa, etc.
Plastic circular or half-moon
 cheese boxes

**Method:**

*Cement the ribbon to the box top edge for hanging. Arrange the greenery and paper figures in the box to create a scene. Cement them in place or stick them into a base of clay.*

# DECORATIONS FOR THE HOUSE

## Candy Tree

**Materials:**

Pins
Candies wrapped in different colored papers
Styrofoam tree

**Method:**

*Stick pin through one end of each candy wrapper and pin to tree. Cover form entirely with brightly colored candies.*

## Gumdrop Tree

**Materials:**

Toothpicks
Green gumdrop leaves cut ½" lengthwise
Styrofoam tree

**Method:**

*Stick a toothpick into each candy, then through the foam tree to pin it there. Put on in overlapping layers, starting at the bottom.*

## Spool Tree

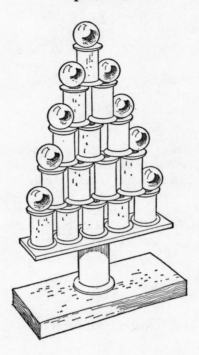

### Materials:

Glue
1 thin, tall empty spool
1 block of wood (3″ by 6″, and 1″ thick)
1 thin strip of wood (1″ by 6″)

15 small empty sewing thread spools
Gold spray paint
9 small gold Christmas balls

### Method:

Glue tall spool to the middle of the block of wood. Glue the thin strip of wood to the top of the tall spool. Woods should be lined up with each other. Glue 15 spools in a pyramid-tree fashion above the thin strip of wood.

When the glue is dry, spray entirely with gold spray. (2 to 3 coats. Dry between sprayings.)

Glue gold balls to the top of each outside spool.

## Tissue Paper Tree

**Materials:**

Colored tissue paper with sequins        Straight pins
    glued on, or colored net          1 Styrofoam tree
Thread

**Method:**

*Cut paper, or net, into oblong strips. Pile a few strips one on top of the other. Tie tightly around the center with thread. Stick a pin in the tied center and pull the tissue paper or net forward into rosette form with the pin sticking out to the rear. Stick rosettes into the tree and cover entirely with rosettes until the tree is colorfully filled out.*

## Christmas Balloons

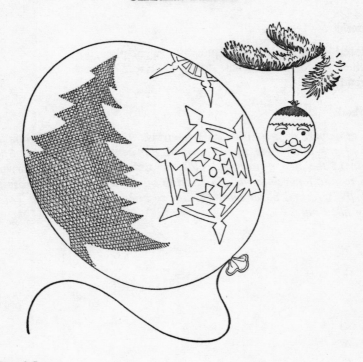

**Materials:**

Colored balloons
Holiday tape

**Method:**

*Blow up balloons and tape in designs—faces, tree, Santa, etc. Hang balloons around the house. If you use small balloons, they can be hung on the Christmas tree.*

## Name Holiday Balloons

**Materials:**

Balloons in different colors
Colored magic markers

**Method:**

*Blow up balloons and tie to keep air in. With colored magic markers gently write, "Merry Christmas, ——."*

## Lattice Balloons

**Materials:**

| | |
|---|---|
| Balloons | Starch |
| String | Pipe cleaners |
| 2 yards mailing string for each balloon | ¾″ red satin ribbon |

**Method:**

*Blow up balloons. Tie each with string for hanging. Dip 2 yards mailing string in a thick starch solution. Starting at the blowing end of the balloon, hold string in position with thumb and wind in lattice fashion around the balloon. Use up all the string, crossing and recrossing the balloon until it is gone. Hang overnight to dry.*

*The next day prick the balloon and withdraw the balloon through the latticework.*

*Use a pipe cleaner for a hanger. Tie a red satin bow at the hanger bottom. (Optional: sequins, glitter, etc., can be added while the string is wet if you wish further decoration.)*

## Wreaths

**Materials:**

Glue

Green felt circles cut to match jar ring size

Rubber jar rings with tabs cut off

Small pine cones

Acorns

Clear lacquer or gold spray paint

Ribbon or gold cord

**Method:**

*Glue felt to each ring to make the back of the wreath. Glue cones and acorns to front of the ring to cover the rubber. When the glue is dry, spray the ring front with clear lacquer or gold spray. Loop with ribbon or cord for hanging.*

## Snowflake Mobile

**Materials:**

Foil

Scissors

Thread

3 pieces of wire

Small embroidery hoop

Small washer

**Method:**

*Fold a square of foil in half. Then in half again. Then once diagonally. Cut the points off and make jagged cuts on the edges. When unfolded a snowflake shape will be revealed. Tie each flake, using varying lengths of thread for hanging.*

*Hang the pieces of wire, equidistantly, around the hoop. Join the wire ends around a small washer so that the mobile can be hung. Tie the snowflake threads onto the hoop at equal distances around.*

## Family Tree

**Materials:**

Construction paper
Magic marker

**Method:**

*Draw this tree form:*

Your name

Your sisters                    Your brothers

Your mother                           Your father

Mother's sisters and brothers        Father's sisters and brothers

Maternal grandparents               Paternal grandparents

*Fill it out with the above information. You can draw Christmas balls or any other designs at the ends of the branches to decorate the tree.*

## Christmas-Designed Light Bulbs

**Materials:**

Light bulbs
Marking felt pens of different colors

**Method:**

*Mark Christmas designs on the bulbs. When the bulbs are used, they will light up the designs.*

## Mirror Decorations

**Materials:**

Decorations cut from colored    Small bells
   felt                         Rubber cement

**Method:**

*Apply decorations and bells to mirror with rubber cement to cre-
ate a Christmasy effect.*

### Christmas Window Shade

**Materials:**

Plain white window shade
Poster paints
Brush

**Method:**

*Draw a Christmas scene on the shade so that when it unrolls the
scene will be displayed, and when it is rolled up it is out of the way.*

## Instant Papier-Mâché Decorations

**Materials:**

Bag of Instant Papier Mâché
(made by Celluclay Company,
available at Sherwin-Williams
stores)
Bowl
Water
Molds or cookie cutters
Liquid detergent

Waxed paper
Fake jewels
Steel screw eyes
Paint (Liquitex Artists' colors
dry quickly)
Varnish
Clear plastic spray

*Instant Papier Mâché adheres to Styrofoam, wood, glass, cans, and wire. It dries in a hard, stony consistency. When it is dry, it can be sanded, sawed, and nailed.*

**Method:**

*Put some Instant Papier Mâché in a large bowl. Add water to the dry material making a moldable dough. Pack with your fingers or a palette knife into a mold moistened with liquid detergent. Or roll out the dough between waxed paper sheets and cut with the wetted edge of cookie cutters or the mold. Or you can sculpt forms free hand.*

*Before drying you can decorate by pressing in fake jewels, or you can combine 2 different-sized shapes. Insert a screw eye for hanging.*

*When dry, paint or varnish. For a brilliant shine spray with clear plastic when dry. You can hurry drying by placing your creation in a 150° oven for a short time.*

# Chapter 14

# MERRY CHRISTMAS IN OTHER LANGUAGES

Would you like to see what Merry Christmas looks like in other languages? Some greetings like *Joyeux Noël* and *Glad Jul* seem familiar, but, no matter how different the words look, they all express the same good wishes.

Armenia  *Schenorhavor Dzenount*

Belgium  *Joyeux Noël* in French-speaking parts of the country, *Vrolijke Kerstmis* where they speak Flemish

Czechoslovakia  *Vesele Vanoce*

Denmark  *Glaedelig Jul*

Finland  *Hauskaa Joulua*

France  *Joyeux Noël*

Germany  *Froehliche Weinachten*

Greece  *Kala Christougena*

Holland  *Zalig Kerstfeest*

Hungary  *Boldog Karacsony*

Ireland  *Nodlaig Nait Cugat* or *Beannact oe' ort*

Italy  *Buon Natale*

Lithuania  *Linksmų Kalēdų*

Mexico  *Feliz Navidad*

Norway  *Gledelig Jul*

Poland  *Wesolych Swiat*

Russia  *S Rozhestvóm Khristóvym*

Spain  *Felices Pascuas*

Sweden  *Glad Jul*

Switzerland  *Joyeux Noël* in French-speaking parts of the country, *Froehliche Weinachten* in German-speaking parts, *Buon Natale* in Italian-speaking parts

Ukraine  *Chrystos Rozdzajetsia Slawyte Jeho*

Yugoslavia  *Sretan Bozic*

# Chapter 15

# INTERNATIONAL MAIL ORDER SHOPPING GUIDE

For convenience I will divide this guide into four areas; food shopping, general shopping, music, and Christmas cards. It is great fun thumbing through this section, and everything from soup to nuts can be found here.

If a company seems to offer something you are interested in, send for their catalogue. You will find it even more fascinating because they can include many items that I cannot fit into my guide. Many brochures have full-color illustrations and are extremely interesting and helpful for times other than Christmas as well.

So, start browsing and have fun!

## Food Shopping

B. Altman & Company, P.O. Box 16, New York, New York 10016
Cookies and tea from all over the world.

Mark Austin, 169 Kingston Road, Wimbledon, London S.W. 19, England
English cakes, candies, cookies, tea.

Barth's Colonial Garden, 270 West Merrick Road, Valley Stream, New York 11582
Jams, jellies, cookies, cakes; candy from other countries.
Also utensils and gifts from abroad.

Cheese-of-all-Nations, 153 Chambers Street, New York, New York 10007
500 cheese varieties listed by country.

Epicures' Club, Elizabeth, New Jersey
Gift packages of delicacies from all over the world.

Ferrara Confectionery Company, 195 Grand Street, New York, New York 10013
Italian cakes, cookies, candies.

Harry and David, Bear Creek Orchards, Medford, Oregon 97501
Delicious fruits and preserves in elaborate Christmas packages.

Kalustyan Orient Export Trading Corporation, 123 Lexington Avenue, New York, New York 10016
Near East and Oriental foods and spices (Turkish, Indian, Chinese, Japanese, etc.).

Lund's Mail Order House, 5314 Eighth Avenue, Brooklyn 20, New York
Scandinavian foods. Odd items such as Swedish mouthwash, Norwegian tobacco.

Manganaro's, 488 Ninth Avenue, New York, New York 10018
All Italian foods, preserves, cakes, candy, cheeses.

Old Country Store, The Nashville House, Nashville, Indiana 47448
All kinds of old-fashioned candies.

Paprikas Weiss, 1546 Second Avenue, New York, New York 10028
Candies, cakes, cookies from many countries. Dolls of all nations. Molds, utensils, food, spices, herbs, preserves.

Perugina, 636 Lexington Avenue, New York, New York 10022
Italian candies.

Plumbridge, 21 East 65th Street, New York, New York 10021
Fruits, candies, nuts, conserves, fruitcakes, all packaged beautifully for Christmas.

H. Roth & Son, 1577 First Avenue, New York, New York 10028
Foods from Europe (Hungarian goulash, Czech frankfurters, strudel dough, Black Forest honey, etc.), herbs and spices, clothing, fortunetelling cards.

S & L Honey Center, 1016 Lexington Avenue, New York, New York 10021
Honeys from around the world. Exotic coffees.

Say-Co Products Company, 14657 Lull Street, Van Nuys, California 91405
Food delicacies and gifts from all over the world.

## General Shopping

Abercrombie & Fitch, Madison Avenue at 45th Street, New York, New York 10017
9 North Wabash, Chicago 2, Illinois 60602
220 Post Street, San Francisco 8, California 94108

A sportsman's heaven. Indoor and outdoor games.

Accent Colonial, Scottsdale, Arizona 85251
Wood-carved (walnut) Christmas greeting "card." Ready to hang on the tree or wall. Comes in form of tree, candle and holly, or Wise Man. Mailing envelope included.

Alexander Sales, 125 Marbledale Road, Tuckahoe, New York 10707
Moscow stacking toy, Spanish *bota*.

Ann Isabel, Department 127, 7840 Rugby Street, Philadelphia, Pennsylvania 19150
Fiberboard playhouse for your cat with wall-to-wall catnip carpeting!

Artisan Galleries, 12 North Haskell, Dallas, Texas 75204
Christmas tree cake pans.

Azuma, 802 Lexington Avenue, New York, New York 10021
Paper flowers, Japanese toys, candles, and lanterns.

Bazaar International, Hanover, Pennsylvania 17331
Dolls, music boxes, jewelry, wood carvings from all over the world.

Bonwit Teller, 5th Avenue at 57th Street, New York, New York 10022
Felt fantasies (topiary tree, wreaths, wall bouquets, garlands) for the tree, centerpieces, window and mantel drapery.

Jean J. Bourgault, St.-Jean-Port-Joli, Province of Quebec, Canada
Monsieur Bourgault's carvings are world renowned. His works are collector's items. They are in museum and private collections throughout the world. Monsieur Bourgault heads the school in St.-Jean-Port-Joli which trains promising young wood carvers in their profession. If you are interested in having a carving or bas-relief made by this artist, write him for information. If you have a sculpture in mind, tell him your idea and the size desired. He will submit a drawing and price to you. If you wish to order, he will then proceed with the work. All work done on approval.

Breck's of Boston, Breck Building, Boston, Massachusetts 02210
Christmas crèche for under the tree. Star of Bethlehem that re-
volves above by means of heat generated by 2 white candles.

Bremen House, 218 East 86th Street, New York, New York 10028
German gift items.

Buffums', Pine Avenue at Broadway, Long Beach, California 90802
Handpainted papier-mâché tree decorated in Mexican style.

Cake Decorators, Blacklick, Ohio 43004
Molds, utensils, decorations, candles. Everything for baking cakes
and cookies.

Camalier & Buckley, 1141 Connecticut Avenue N.W., Washing-
ton, D.C. 20036
Gifts for the entire family and home, from the United States and
Europe.

Campbell Gifts, 11 South Wyoming Avenue, Ardmore, Pennsylvania 19003
7-inch-tall *Mad* artist pencil holder with 10 colored pencils.

Casual Living, Stony Hill, Bethel, Connecticut 06801
Carve-it-yourself pipe to be made from a block of genuine
Corsican briar; Twelve Days of Christmas tiles; railroad spike
statuettes for golfers; Danish collector's Christmas spoons; scrimshaw ornaments; personalized and designed outdoor mailboxes;
Lucite blocks for snapshot framing; scrimshaw bracelets, earrings,
brooches, blazer buttons; silver charms from Denmark; folding
wine rack; collector rocks (or your own) embedded in Lucite; the
complete fondue set; pen with a built-in light; cathedral windows
(transparencies embedded in Lucite for use as paperweight or
display).

Cepelia, 5 East 57th Street, New York, New York 10019
Polish arts and crafts items.

Charm & Treasure, 1201 Sixth Avenue, New York, New York 10036
Noël charms (gold or silver) in tree form, Santa, or Merry
Christmas.

Children's Workbench, 217 East 51st Street, New York, New
York 10022
Children's furniture from Sweden.

Clymer's of Bucks County, Point Pleasant, Pennsylvania 18950
Willow trees for holiday trimming.

Crown Craft, Mt. Hope Place, Bronx, New York 10453
International dolls dressed in costume (eyes close, arms and legs move, over 3″ high).

Eunice Curtis, 14407 Southeast 55th Street, Bellevue, Washington 98004
Holiday centerpiece kit (dried arrangement), pine cone tree kit.

Dennison's Party Bazaar, 390 Fifth Avenue, New York, New York 10018
Large collection of Christmas decorations.

Downs, Department 1412-J, Evanston, Illinois 60204
Gay Danish straw Christmas tree or mantel ornaments (stars, bells, angels) with bright ribbon or berry color accents; Twelve Days of Christmas dolls ready for hanging on tree, mantel, or window (gift-boxed); white feathery doves, cardinals; Swedish tree skirt; pine cone angels; Christmas spoons; German brass Christmas ornaments (snowflake, angels, Santa, animal mobiles).

Elder Craftsmen, 850 Lexington Avenue, New York, New York 10022
Felt angels; satin and jeweled Christmas balls; Santa stockings with belled toes; sequined, pearl-dotted Christmas balls.

Emgee Corporation, 3210 Koapaka, Honolulu, Hawaii 96819
Handmade wooden tree ornaments.

European Gift House, 70 Demloostraat, Amsterdam, Holland
Dolls from Holland and Switzerland; wooden shoes; lederhosen from Austria; gifts for children.

Fabrics 'Round the World, Inc., 270 West 38th Street, New York, New York 10018
Fabrics from all over the world.

Stephen Faller, Ltd., Galway, Ireland
Irish jewelry, charms, souvenirs.

Mark Farmer Company, 11427 San Pablo Avenue, El Cerrito, California 94532
Dolls from all over the world—kits, clothes, stands, miniature furniture; imported Christmas cards; wooden crèche figures.

Foster House, Department 112-9237, Peoria, Illinois 61601
Golden stick-ons in many designs for using in gift wrapping; paper tablecloths; Three Kings candlesticks; many gift items and decorations.

Helen Gallagher-Foster House, 6523 North Galena Road, Peoria, Illinois 61601
Party favors; decorations, gifts; utensils; gift wrapping; many foreign items; angel tree lights with bulbs; papier-mâché angels.

Georgetown Coffee House, 1330 Wisconsin Avenue, Northwest, Washington, D.C. 20007
Gingerbread house (completely edible).

Gifts, Gadgets, Gems, 915 South Scenic Drive, Springfield, Missouri 65802
Fascinating blown-glass miniatures.

Gifts from the Heart, Scotia, New York 12302
Decorated Danish paper Christmas trees; manger mobiles.

Gifts Galore, Box 272, Department G-73, Culver City, California 90231
Inexpensive Yuletide jewelry (pins, earrings).

Gina & Selma Inc., 1048 Lexington Avenue, New York, New York 10021
Table-top German Christmas tree with glass ornaments, real candles, wax angel on top, small crib under tree.

Go Fly A Kite Shop, 1613 Second Avenue, New York, New York 10028
Kites, books on kites from all over the world.

Marcel Guay, St.-Jean-Port-Joli, Province of Quebec, Canada
Monsieur Guay carves a variety of French Provincial figures and animals in various original poses and in varying sizes. He also carves crèches. He has other artisans working in his shop whose works and styles are distinctive. I particularly recommend the young boy figures created and carved by Maurice Harvey. His statue in my own collection is one of my favorite carvings. You may write for a catalogue and price list.

Hampshire Company, Piqua, Ohio 45356
Canopied 4-poster dog bed for the dog who has everything!

Here's How Company, 15 West 26th Street, New York, New York 10010
Imported gifts for the house.

High Towers, 105 North Hudson Street, Oklahoma City, Oklahoma 73102
Colorful, stuffed hand-knitted birds from Peru.

Hildegarde Studios, 597 Farmington Avenue, Hartford, Connecticut 06105
Hummel Nativity scene; other Hummel Christmas figurines.

The Jamaica Silversmith, 50 Delancey Street, New York, New York 10002
Classic sterling silver crosses (English, French, Florentine, Cellini).

Georg Jensen, 667 Fifth Avenue, New York, New York 10022
Clay musicians from Peru.

Miles Kimball, Kimball Building, Oshkosh, Wisconsin 54902
Decorations; favors; huge lollipops; toys; games; candles; gifts.

Kitchens of Sara Lee, Box 799, Chicago, Illinois 60677
Miniature fruitcakes in Christmas gift tins.

Kontiki Mart, P.O. Box 7566, Honolulu, Hawaii 96821
Large Hawaii-print stuffed animals that are very gay.

Lord & Taylor, Fifth Avenue and 38th Street, New York, New York 10018
Hand-blown glass deer; felt gingerbread men and gingerbread houses and animals; elegant beaded eggs; brass bells from India; tin butterflies from Mexico; burlap angels; tailed tin comet from Mexico; papier-mâché figures; wooden clowns.

Madison House, Nursery Division, Box 454, Fort Myers, Florida 33902
Potted trees (indoor holly, Christmas cactus, miniature orange, gardenia, lemon, lime, hibiscus, palm, coffee).

Mahopac Country Store, Route 6 and Baldwin Place Road, Mahopac, New York 10505
Unusual polychromed baked bread ornaments from Ecuador (animals, costumed dolls); foreign decorations and gifts; German Black Forest hand-carved Nativity characters; Mexican ornaments and gifts.

Maid of Scandinavia, 3245 Raleigh Avenue, Minneapolis, Minnesota 55416
One of the most beautiful and complete catalogues for all party goods. Utensils; molds; paper goods; favors; decorations; arts and crafts materials; charms; candlemaking supplies; party cloths; napkins; centerpieces; Swiss lollipops; marzipan candy in shapes; rainbow sugar.

Elizabeth McCaffrey, Northport, New York 11768
Santa napkin holders.

Mr. Christmas, Christmas Creations, 212 Fifth Avenue, New York,
New York 10010
Many well-made novel Christmas decorations for tree, house, and
gifts. Foreign decorations.

Neiman-Marcus, Dallas, Texas 75200
Christmas gift catalogue full of fantastic gifts. Jewelry, clothes,
gifts.

Northwest Corner Store, Longview 2, Washington 98632
Boxed holly and mistletoe; pine cones; greens.

Old Mexico Shop, Patio 2, Santa Fe, New Mexico
Red pepper wreaths; metal Christmas trees in original creations
complete with candles; dolls; toys.

Pampered Kitchens, Inc., 21 East 10th Street, New York, New York
10003
Unusual kitchen gifts to make life easy for the cook.

The Patio, Box 25, Highland Park, Illinois 60036
Mexican marionettes; bushel of Far East toys; gift-filled Santa
Piñata; rattan rocking horse supports 300 pounds.

Piñata Party, 129 Macdougal Street, New York, New York 10012
Straw Santa, sunburst, angel, deer from Ecuador.

The Pink Sleigh, Route 153, Westbrook, Connecticut 06498
Wire-framed twistable Herr and Frau Kringle.

Poco Imports, 2617 East Third Avenue, Denver, Colorado 80206
Mexican gifts.

Nancy Resetar, P.O. Box 781, Port Chester, New York 10573
Child's drawing reproduced in full color on ceramics.

H. Roth & Son, 1577 First Avenue, New York, New York 10028
Foreign dolls; chocolate Christmas tree ornaments; foreign
candy; unusual molds; cake-decorating and cookie-cutter sets;
cookie-decorating rolling pin; beeswax; German Christmas cookies; gingerbread and Santa figures; chocolate Christmas tree figures; Hungarian cakes, cookies, and candies for Christmas; kitchen
gadgets from Europe.

Royal Seal, 414 East Wayne, Fort Wayne, Indiana 46802
Musical Nativity scene.

Santons de Provence, Pleasant Point Road, Topsham, Maine 04086
Clay Christmas figures for the crèche.

Max Schling Seedsmen, 270 West Merrick Road, Valley Stream,
New York 11582
Exotic bird feeders; gourmet herb garden from around the world;
giant photo posters made from snapshots; Kolor Kindler for
rainbow flames in the fireplace; magic clay that bakes in a home
oven; origami paper-folding kit; perfumed pen for scented letters;
sterling silver charms from Denmark; chairs from Spain; real
rosebuds and holly preserved in 24-carat gold (pins, earrings);
Aztec bark paintings; buffalo sandals from India; brass betel box
from India; Scandinavian pipe racks; German Black Forest cuckoo
clocks; shamrock seeds from Ireland; papier-mâché kit; whittling
kit; chocolate dishes and cordial cups.

William Schmidt, Karl Johans Gate 41, Oslo, Norway.
Norwegian clothes; hand carvings.

F. A. O. Schwarz, 745 Fifth Avenue, New York, New York 10022
Large selection of foreign toys, games; arts and crafts materials;
origami kits; puppets; dolls; costumes.

Scottish Products, Inc., 24 East 60th Street, New York, New
York 10022
Gifts; clothing; jewelry, toys; bagpipes.

Seabon, 54 East 54th Street, New York, New York 10022
Carved wooden Danish flower tree; Danish wooden hanging ornaments.

Sears, Roebuck & Company, Philadelphia, Pennsylvania 19100
The special Christmas book has many foreign items (cookies,
cakes, cheese trays, candies, *piñatas,* gifts); Christmas tree lights;
indoor and outdoor lights; toys; games; records; costumes.

Serendipity 3, 225 East 60th Street, New York, New York 10022
Mad gifts from around the world.

Shopping International, Inc., 25 North Main Street, White River
Junction, Vermont 05001
Variety of international gifts (Mexican tree ornaments; Mexican
wood carvings; German *Zwiefalten* angel; Fred the Nutcracker;
German hand-carved ivory edelweiss brooch and earrings; colored
tin Christmas tree ornaments; tin Christmas trees painted with

birds and flowers and having candleholders; hand-carved camel caravans from Bethlehem; sterling crusader crosses).

Spencer Gifts, Spencer Building, Atlantic City, New Jersey 08404
Gift-wrap items; personalized pencils; many gift items; liquor-flavored lollipops; tree decorations with lights.

Sponholz, 850 Seventh Avenue, New York, New York 10019
Unusual musical and mechanical gifts.

Sunset House, 81 Sunset Building, Beverly Hills, California 90213
Brass card tree; musical madonna and angel; gift-wrap items; many gift items from around the world; Yuletide trimmings (holly leaves and berries); life-sized plastic Santa ready to stuff; fast-wrapping gift boxes; pixie-headed candy-striped pencils.

Tartan Gift Shop, 96 & 96A Princes Street, Edinburgh 2, Scotland
Scottish jewelry; dolls; gifts; clothing; miniature bagpipes.

Taylor Gifts, 211 Conestoga Road, Wayne, Pennsylvania 19087
Packages of clear plastic disposable glasses in various sizes; grandmother rings with grandchildren's birthstones in them; pins of real roses dipped in 24-carat gold, made in Austria; artificial peonies made in France; sterling silver cake testers; 100 perfume vials of various scents; Lippizanner scarves from Austria; sundial bracelets; miniature coin-operated jukeboxes; real fishbowl neck-laces; British pub jugs; revolving Santa music boxes; special pipe ashtrays; elephant-ear wallets; currency converters; world-wide electricity converters; crate of Danish food; Yale travel locks; guaranteed pearl oyster in a can; 3-dimensional jigsaw puzzles; fortunetelling cards; Turkish water pipes.

Adalbert and Lorraine Thibault, St.-Jean-Port-Joli, County L' Islet, Province of Quebec, Canada
Monsieur and Madame Thibault are a charming couple whose wood carvings you may have seen in shops in Canada and the United States. They carve a variety of items created in natural wood or with painted finish. You can order the traditional French Provincial figures (2½″ and up); wall plaques; birds; bracelets with cameo French Provincial figures; cuff links; earrings; pins; carved corks; boats; letter openers; and bookmarks. All are pro-duced in finest detail in wood. Write for information and prices.

Tillalla, P.O. Box 484, New York, New York 10021
Swedish needlecraft kits; Cum Rya rugs; wall hangings and cushions.

Toymaker of Williamsburg, P.O. Box 2035, Williamsburg, Virginia 23185
Revolving Swiss music boxes of carved wood with Christmas scenes on them, made in Italy; toys.

Treasure-Trove, P.O. Box 2440 Grand Central Station, New York, New York 10017
Befana on a broomstick from Italy.

Windfall, 185 Adams Street, Bedford Hills, New York 10517
Unusual items from all over the world: (hand-painted tree ornaments; rocking horses; reindeer; Santas; trees; stockings; angels; snowmen).

World Arts, Box 577, Wilmington 38, California 90744
Stained-glass chandelier kit.

## Music

Berliner's Music Shop, 154 Fourth Avenue, New York, New York 10003
Records of music from many countries (for listening, folk dancing, party games).

## Christmas Cards

Breck's, 100 Breck Building, Boston 10, Massachusetts 02110
Nice selection of cards for the season.

Brooklyn Museum, Eastern Parkway, Brooklyn, New York 11238
Cards designed by artists of many countries.

Miles Kimball, 186 Bond Street, Oshkosh, Wisconsin 54901
Attractive cards for the holidays.

UNICEF, United Nations, First Avenue and 45th Street, New York, New York 10017
Cards of greeting designed in many nations.

# INDEX